OUR DAILY BREAD

With Daily Liturgical Readings
JANUARY / NEW YEAR EDITION

FR JOHN DAMIAN ADIZIE
(Apostle of Divine Mercy)

OUR DAILY BREAD

With Daily Liturgical Readings

JANUARY / NEW YEAR EDITION

FR JOHN DAMIAN ADIZIE
(Apostle of Divine Mercy)

Plush Prints
and Paper Works

Copyright © 2025
Rev. Fr. John Damian Adizie
(Apostle of Divine Mercy)

ISBN:
9798305435627

All right reserved. No part of this publication may be reproduced, stored in a retrieval system, or transmitted, in any form or by any means, electronic, mechanical, photocopying, recording, or otherwise, without the prior written permission of the author

Printed by:
Plush Prints & Paperworks
Shop 18, Goshen Plaza
16 Ewasede Street, Off Agbado Street,
Off First East Circular Rd. Benin City.
09036413739

DEDICATION

This book is dedicated to the entire members of the Altar of Divine Mercy Eucharistic Adoration, especially the Daily Online worshippers of the Altar of Divine Mercy Eucharistic Adoration @ facebook and YouTube Channel, to all our viewers at the Altar of Divine Mercy Satellite Television and to you my dear reader.

INTRODUCTION

Your prayers for daily Bread have just been answered! Our Daily Bread is an answer to the Lord's Prayer "Give Us this Day Our Daily Bread" (Matthew 6:11). Our Daily Bread is a daily spiritual Nourishment. Take, Eat and be nourished on a daily basis.

In the book of Numbers 6:22 the Lord said to Moses: Speak to Aaron and his sons, saying, *"Thus you shall bless the Israelites."* The family of Aaron is the Priestly family. God wants His priests to bless His people, if possible, on a daily basis.

Our Daily Bread is a daily Prophetic Message and blessings. Apart from the daily prophetic blessings, this book also contains the daily liturgical readings, with Saints of the day.

As a Priest of the Most High God, I want you to succeed in all your endeavours. As you go through this book daily your days will be blessed. Whatever you lay your hands shall be blessed. Your going out and your coming in shall be blessed and it shall be well with you in Jesus name – Amen!

Contents

Dedication v
Introduction vii

January 1: You are Blessed! 1
January 2: You will have eternal Life 7
January 3: You are God's Favoured Child.................. 12
January 4: You will not be deceived again! 16
January 5: You are a Channel of God's Glory! 22
January 6: You are Greater than those in the World ... 30
January 7: You are a Channel of Love 35
January 8: God Abides in You! 39
January 9: Hatred is over! 43
January 10: You are Destined for Eternal Life 47
January 11: Whatever You Ask You shall Receive 51
January 12: Baptism of Divine Consolation 57
January 13: You now have a Direct Access to God 66
January 14: You are crowed with Glory and Honour... 70
January 15: You shall be Delivered from
              Lifelong Bondage 75
January 16: You shall Hear the Voice of the Lord 80
January 17: You shall Experience God's Rest 84
January 18: You Shall Receive Grace and Mercy 89
January 19: You shall be Vindicated 95
January 20: You have been Called by God 103
January 21: God will Bless and Multiply You 108
January 22: You are a Priest Forever 113

January 23: Jesus will surely Save You! 118
January 24: You are a Covenantal Child 123
January 25: Your Past is Over!... 128
January 26: Your Period of Weeping is Over! 133
January 27: As You Wait for Christ You will be Saved. 143
January 28: You will do God's Will 148
January 29: Your sins will be remembered no more 153
January 30: Your God is a Faithful God 159
January 31: You shall Live by Faith........................ 163

JANUARY 1
YOU ARE BLESSED!

Daily Bread

Happy New year and Welcome to the Year of jubilee! Welcome to the year of celebration! Welcome to the year of Favour! And welcome to the Year of Blessings! The Lord has just ordered me to bless you.

In the book of Numbers 6:22-27 the Lord said to Moses, "Say to Aaron and his sons, thus you shall bless the sons of Israel: you shall say to them, The LORD bless you and keep you: The LORD make his face to shine upon you, and be gracious to you: The LORD lift up his countenance upon you, and give you peace. "So shall they put my name upon the sons of Israel, And I will bless them."

Child of God, as the face of God continue to shine on you, I hereby cancel every curses you must have inherited either from your parents or your family. Parental curses are cancelled in Jesus name! Inherited curses are cancelled in Jesus name! Ancestral curses are cancelled in Jesus name!

I release more blessings upon you! I bless your home! Your business is blessed! Your family is blessed! You vocation and your marital life is blessed! Your academics is blessed! Whatever you lay your hands shall be blessed!

I wish you success in all your endeavours! Failure and disappointment will never be your portion. Throughout this year you will celebrate and you will be celebrated. Goodness and mercy shall follow you all the days of your life and you shall remain in the presence of God forever and ever – Amen!

Mary, Mother of God- Pray for Us!
Happy New Year!

Daily Readings:
SOLEMNITY OF MARY, MOTHER OF GOD
Entrance Antiphon
Hail, Holy Mother, who gave birth to the King who rules heaven and earth forever.

Or: Cf. Is 9:1.5; Lk 1:33
Today a light will shine upon us, for the Lord is born for us; and he will be called Wondrous God, Prince of peace, Father of future ages: and his reign will be without end.

Collect:
O God, who through the fruitful virginity of Blessed Mary bestowed on the human race the grace of eternal salvation, grant, we pray, that we may experience the intercession of her, through whom we were found worthy to receive the author of life, our Lord Jesus Christ, your Son Who lives and reigns with you in the unity of the Holy Spirit, one God, for ever and ever.

FIRST READING   Numbers 6:22-27
"They shall put my name upon the people of Israel, and I will bless them."
The Lord said to Moses, "Say to Aaron and his sons, thus you shall bless the sons of Israel: you shall say to them, The LORD bless you and keep you: The LORD make his face to shine upon you, and be gracious to you: The LORD lift up his countenance upon you, and give you peace. "So shall they put my name upon the sons of Israel, And I will bless them."
The word of the Lord.

RESPONSORIAL PSALM
Psalm 67:2-3.5.6 and 8 (R. 2a)
R. O God, be gracious and bless us.
O God, be gracious and bless us

and let your face shed its light upon us.
So will your ways be known upon earth
and all nations learn your salvation. R.

Let the nations be glad and shout for joy,
with uprightness you rule the peoples;
you guide the nations on earth. R.

Let the peoples praise you, O God;
let all the peoples praise you.
May God still give us his blessing
that all the ends of the earth may revere him. R.

SECOND READING

"God sent forth his Son, born of a woman."
Brethren: When the time had fully come, God sent forth his Son, born of woman, born under the law, to redeem those who were under the law, so that we might receive adoption as sons. And because you are sons, God has sent the Spirit of his Son into our hearts, crying, "Abba! Father!" So, through God you are no longer a slave but a son, and if a son then an heir.
The word of the Lord.
Gospel Acclamation: Hebrews 1:1-2
V. Alleluia. R. Alleluia. V. In many and various ways

God spoke of old to our fathers by the prophets; but in these last days he has spoken to us by a Son. **R.** Alleluia.

GOSPEL   Luke 2:16-21
"They found Mary and Joseph, and the baby . . . And at the end of eight days, he was called Jesus."
At that time: The shepherds went with haste to Bethlehem, and found Mary and Joseph, and the baby lying in a manger. And when they saw it they made known the saying which had been told them concerning this child; and all who heard it wondered at what the shepherds told them. But Mary kept all these things, pondering them in her heart. And the shepherds returned, glorifying and praising God for all they had heard and seen, as it had been told them. And at the end of eight days, when he was circumcised, he was called Jesus, the name given by the angel before he was conceived in the womb.
The Gospel of the Lord.

Prayer over the Offerings
O God, who in your kindness begin all good things and bring them to fulfilment, grant to us, who find joy in the Solemnity of the holy Mother of God, that, just as we glory in the beginnings of your grace, so

one day we may rejoice in its completion.
Through Christ our Lord.

Communion Antiphon   Heb. 13:8
Jesus Christ is the same yesterday, today, and for ever.

Prayer after Communion
We have received this heavenly Sacrament with joy, O Lord: grant, we pray, that it may lead us to eternal life, for we rejoice to proclaim the blessed ever-Virgin Mary Mother of your Son and Mother of the Church. Through Christ our Lord.

JANUARY 2
YOU WILL HAVE ETERNAL LIFE

Daily Bread

Child of God, the Truth is about to set you free! God is about to deliver you from the spirit of the antichrist! You are about to be connected to the path of eternal life. Who then is a liar? Who is an antichrist?

A liar according to 1 John 2:22-28 is "He who denies that Jesus is the Christ. This is the antichrist, he who denies the Father and the Son. Anyone who denies the Son does not have the Father." Child of God, as you renounce the spirit of lies and the spirit of antichrist, you are hereby declared free in the name of God the Father, God the Son and God the Holy Spirit - Amen!

Do you really want to inherit eternal life? And do you want to know the secret of Eternal Life? According to St. John, "He who confesses the Son has the Father also. Let what you heard from the beginning abide in you. If what you heard from the beginning abides in you, then you will abide in the Son and in the Father. And this is what he has promised us, eternal life." Your knowledge of our Lord Jesus Christ and that of God the Father is what eternal life is all about.

As you deepen your knowledge of Christ and your love for God the Father you will surely have eternal life and it shall be well with you in Jesus name – Amen!

St. Basil the Great – Pray for Us!

Daily Readings:
CHRISTMAS TIME

FIRST READING   1 John 2:22-8

What you heard from the beginning abides in you
Beloved: Who is the liar but he who denies that Jesus is the Christ? This is the antichrist, he who denies the Father and the Son. Anyone who denies the Son does not have the Father. He who confesses the Son has the Father also. Let what you heard from the beginning abide in you. If what you heard from the beginning abides in you, then you will abide in the Son and in the Father. And this is what he has

promised us, eternal life. I write this to you about those who would deceive you; but the anointing which you received from him abides in you, and you have no need that any one should teach you; as his anointing teaches you about everything, and is true, and is no lie, just as it has taught you, abide in him. And now, little children, abide in him, so that when he appears we may have confidence and not shrink from him in shame at his coming.
The word of the Lord

RESPONSORIAL PSALM
Psalm 98:1, 2-3ab, 3cd-4 (R. 3cd)
R. All the ends of the earth have seen the salvation of our God.
O sing a new song to the Lord,
For he has worked wonders.
His right hand and his holy arm
Have brought salvation. R

The Lord has made known his salvation,
Has shown his deliverance to the nations
He has remembered his merciful love
And his truth for the house of Israel. R

All the ends of the earth have seen

The salvation of our God.
Shout to the Lord, all the earth;
break forth into joyous song,
and sing out your praise. R

ALLELUIA **Hebrews 1:1-2**

V. Alleluia. R. Alleluia. *V.* In many and various ways God spoke of old to our fathers by the prophets; but in these last days he has spoken to us by a Son. **R. Alleluia.**

GOSPEL John 1:19-28

"He who comes after me."

This is the testimony of John, when the Jews sent priests and Levites from Jerusalem to ask him, "Who are you?" He confessed, he did not deny, but confessed, "I am not the Christ" And they asked him, "What then? Are you Elijah?" He said, "I am not." "Are you the prophet?" And he answered, "No." They said to him then, "Who are you? Let us have an answer for those who sent us. What do you say about yourself?" He said, "I am the voice of one crying in the wilderness, 'Make straight the way of the Lord,' as the prophet Isaiah said." Now they had been sent from the Pharisees. They asked him, "Then why are you baptizing, if you are neither the Christ, nor

Elijah, nor the prophet?" John answered them, "I baptise with water; but among you stands one whom you do not know, even he who comes after me, the thong of whose sandal I am not worthy to untie." This took place in Bethany beyond the Jordan, where John was baptizing.
The Gospel of the Lord

JANUARY 3

YOU ARE GOD'S FAVOURED CHILD

Daily Bread

Who says you are nobody? Who says you have no identity? Has anyone tried to disregard you? Worry not! Your true identity is about to be restored!

1 John 3:1-6 declares "Beloved See what love the Father has given us, that we should be called children of God; and so we are. The reason why the world does not know us is that it did not know him." From this passage your true identity has been revealed. The first thing you must know about yourself is that you are a beloved child of God.

You are not just a child of God; you are also destined to share in the glory of our Lord Jesus Christ. As St. John rightly declares, "Beloved, we are God's children now; it does not yet appear what we shall be, but we know that when he appears we shall be like him, for we shall see him as he is. And every one who thus hopes in him purifies himself as he is pure." As you avoid sin God will purify your soul and He will grant you eternal life and it shall be well with you in Jesus name – Amen!

Holy Name of Jesus – Have Mercy on Us!

Happy Feast of the Holy Name of Jesus!

Daily Readings:
CHRISTMAS TIME

FIRST READING   1 John 2:29—3:6

Anyone who abides in him does not sin.
Beloved: If you know that God is righteous, you may be sure that everyone who does right is born of him. See what love the Father has given us, that we should be called children of God; and so we are. The reason why the world does not know us is that it did not know him. Beloved, we are God's children now; **it** does not yet appear what we shall he, but we know that when he appears we shall be like him, for we shall see him as he is. And everyone who thus hopes in him purifies himself as he is pure. Everyone who commits sin is guilty of lawlessness; sin is lawlessness. You know that he appeared to take away sins, and in him there is no sin. Anyone who abides in him does not sin; anyone who sins has not

seen him, nor has he known him.
The word of the Lord

RESPONSORIAL PSALM
Psalm 98:1, 3cd-4, 5-6 (R. 3cd)
R. All the ends of the earth have seen the salvation of our God.
O sing a new song to the Lord,
for he has worked wonders.
His right hand and his holy arm
have brought salvation. R

All the ends of the earth have seen
the salvation of our God.
Shout to the Lord, all the earth;
break forth into joyous song,
and sing out your praise. R

Sing psalms to the Lord with the harp,
with the harp and the sound of song.
With trumpets and the sound of the horn,
raise a shout before the King, the Lord. R

Gospel Acclamation: John 1:14a, 12ac
V. Alleluia. R. Alleluia.
V. The Word became flesh and dwelt among us. To

all who received him, He gave power to become children of God. **R. Alleluia.**

GOSPEL   John 1:29-34

"Behold, the Lamb of God."

The next day John saw Jesus coming toward him, and said, "Behold, the Lamb of God, who takes away the sin of the world! This is he of whom I said, 'After me comes a man who ranks before me, for he was before me.' I myself did not know him; but for this I came baptizing with water, that he might be revealed to Israel." And John bore witness, "I saw the Spirit descend as a dove from heaven and remain on him. I myself did not know him; but he who sent me to baptise with water said to me, 'He on whom you see the Spirit descend and remain, this is he who baptises with the Holy Spirit.' And I have seen and have borne witness that this is the Son of God."
The Gospel of the Lord

January 4

You Will Not Be Deceived Again!

Daily Bread

God has come to destroy the works of satan. He has come to abolish all the plans of your enemies. He has come to destroy their evil agendas. Every spirit of deception is about to be destroyed! You will not be deceived again!

1 John 3:7-10 declares, "Little children, let no one deceive you..." Who is a deceiver? A deceiver is one who leads others astray. He is one who induces others into error. A deceiver is a liar!

Revelation 12:9-10 described the devil as a deceiver "So, the great dragon was cast out, that serpent of old, called the Devil and Satan, who deceives the whole world; he was cast to the earth, and his angels were cast out with him." The devil is indeed the father of all deceivers! He is the father of all liars.

The Gospel of John 8:44 described him as a

murderer and a chronic liar: "You are of *your* father the devil, and the desires of your father you want to do. He was a murderer from the beginning, and does not stand in the truth, because there is no truth in him. When he speaks a lie, he speaks from his own *resources,* for he is a liar and the father of it." The devil, according to our Lord Jesus Christ, is not just a liar he is also the father of liars. He is the architect of lies.

The book of Genesis 3:1-7 shows the true colour of the devil as a deceiver. He came to Eve and asked, "Has God indeed said, 'You shall not eat of every tree of the garden'?" And the woman said to the serpent, "We may eat the fruit of the trees of the garden; but of the fruit of the tree which *is* in the midst of the garden, God has said, 'You shall not eat it, nor shall you touch it, lest you die.'"

Then the serpent said to the woman, "You will not surely die. For God knows that in the day you eat of it your eyes will be opened and you will be like God, knowing good and evil." But this is not true! Do you now see the reason why the devil is described as a liar?

So when the woman saw that the tree was good for food, that it was pleasant to the eyes, and a tree desirable to make one wise, she took of its fruit and ate. She also gave to her husband and he ate. Then the eyes of both of them were opened, and they knew that they *were* naked... Imagine! Has the devil not succeeded in deceiving them? Try to visualize how many people that have allowed the devil to deceive them.

A sinner is one who allows himself to be deceived by the devil. As 1 John 3:7-10 rightly declares, "He who commits sin is of the devil; for the devil has sinned from the beginning." Any time you commit sin you are simply identifying with the devil. A righteous person is one who does what is right. May God give you the grace to live righteous and upright life!

Finally, 1 John 3:8 declares, "The reason the Son of God appeared was to destroy the works of the devil." Child of God, as long as you remain connected to our Lord Jesus Christ the yoke of deception is broken! All the evil works of satan are destroyed. You are hereby declared free in the name of God the Father, Son and Holy Spirit – Amen!

St. Elizabeth Ann Seton – Pray for Us!

Daily Readings:
CHRISTMAS TIME

FIRST READING   I John 3:7-10

"He cannot sin because he is born of God."
Little children, let no one deceive you. He who does right is righteous, as he is righteous. He who commits sin is of the devil; for the devil has sinned from the beginning. The reason the Son of God appeared was to destroy the works of the devil. Any one born of God does not commit sin; for God's seed abides in him, and he cannot sin because he is born of God. By this it may be seen who are the children of God, and who are the children of the devil: whoever does not do right is not of God, nor he who does not love his brother.
The word of the Lord

RESPONSORIAL PSALM

Psalm 98:1, 7-9ab, 9cd (R. 3cd)

R. All the ends of the earth have seen the salvation of our God.
O sing a new song to the Lord,
for he has worked wonders.
His right hand and his holy arm
have brought salvation. R

Let the sea and all within it thunder;
the world, and those who dwell in it.
Let the rivers clap their hands,
and the hills ring out their joy
at the presence of the Lord, for he comes,
he comes to judge the earth. R

He will judge the world with justice,
and the peoples with fairness. R

Gospel Acclamation: Hebrews 1:1-2
V. Alleluia. **R.** Alleluia.
V. In many and various ways God spoke of old by the prophets; but in these last days he has spoken to us by a Son. **R.** Alleluia.

GOSPEL John 1:35-42
"We have found the Messiah."
The next day again John was standing with two of his disciples; and he looked at Jesus as he walked, and said, "Behold, the Lamb of God!" The two disciples heard him say this, and they followed Jesus. Jesus turned, and saw them following, and said to them, "What do you seek?" And they said to him, "Rabbi" (which means Teacher), "where are you staying?" He said to them, "Come and see." They

came and saw where he was staying; and they stayed with him that day, for it was about the tenth hour. One of the two who heard John speak, and followed him, was Andrew, Simon Peter's brother. He first found his brother Simon, and said to him, "We have found the Messiah" (which means Christ) He brought him to Jesus. Jesus looked at him, and said, "So you are Simon the son of John? You shall be called Cephas" (which means Peter).
The Gospel of the Lord

January 5

You Are a Channel of God's Glory!

Daily Bread

Today is the Epiphany of our Lord Jesus Christ. Epiphany is a moment of glorious manifestation or revelation. It is the divine manifestation of our Lord Jesus Christ to the Gentiles and the world as a whole.

The three major Epiphanies of our Lord Jesus after his birth were the visit of the Magi, the Baptism of our Lord Jesus Christ and the Wedding at Cana in Galilee. These were the three major occasions where the true and divine identity of our Lord Jesus Christ was made manifest.

The visit of the Magi was a remarkable event in the life of our Lord Jesus Christ. They came to Jerusalem saying, "Where is he who has been born king of the Jews? For we have seen his star in the East, and have come to worship him." They not only recognized Jesus as the King of the Jews they also said they have come to worship Him. Worship here is a divine attribute.

During his Baptism God the Father's voice was heard, saying, "This is My beloved Son, in whom I am well pleased." With this declaration it is obvious that Jesus is not just the son of Joseph and Mary, He is the Beloved Son of the Most High God. He is the Second Person of the Blessed Trinity.

The peak of His divine manifestation was what happened at Cana in Galilee when our Lord Jesus Christ performed his first miracle at Cana in Galilee. After turning Water into Wine the gospel of John 2:11 clearly affirm that "This is the beginning of signs Jesus did in Cana of Galilee, and manifested His glory; and His disciples believed in Him." Faith in Christ Jesus is indeed the essence of Epiphany.

Child of God, it is your turn to receive! Be ready to receive your own Epiphany. Be ready to experience Divine manifestation. Through this message God is going to manifest His glory in your life, your family and in your nation.

The book of Isaiah 60:1-6 declares, "Arise, shine; for your light has come, and the glory of the Lord has risen upon you." Child of God, anywhere you are right now, rise up on your feet begin to shine. Begin to celebrate! For indeed your light has come! Your period of darkness is over!

"For behold, darkness shall cover the earth, and thick darkness shall cover the people; but the Lord will arise upon you, and his glory will be seen upon you." Oh yes, you are a channel of God's glory! Through you people around you will see the glory of God. In fact, nations shall walk by your light, and kings in the brightness of your rising.

You are not just a channel of glory you are also a channel of Light. As our Lord Jesus Christ declares in Matthew 5:14-16 "You are the light of the world. A city that is set on a hill cannot be hidden. Nor do they light a lamp and put it under a basket, but on a lampstand, and it gives light to all *who are* in the house. Let your light so shine before men, that they may see your good works and glorify your Father in heaven." Child of God, your light must shine!

As your light continues to shine, "you shall see and be radiant, your heart shall thrill and rejoice; because the abundance of the sea shall be turned to you, the wealth of the nations shall come to you." And it shall be well with you in Jesus name – Amen!

Happy Epiphany of our Lord Jesus Christ!

Daily Readings:
EPIPHANY OF THE LORD

Entrance Antiphon   Mal 3:1; 1 Chr29:12
Behold, the Lord, the Mighty One, has come; and kingship is in his grasp, and power and dominion.

Collect
O God, who on this day revealed your Only Begotten Son to the nations by the guidance of a star, grant in your mercy, that we, who know you already by faith, may be brought to behold the beauty of your sublime glory. Through our Lord…

FIRST READING   Isaiah 60:1-6
"The glory of the Lord has risen upon you."
Arise, shine; for your light has come, and the glory of the Lord has risen upon you. For behold, darkness shall cover the earth, and thick darkness the peoples; but the Lord will arise upon you, and his glory will be seen upon you. And nations shall walk by your light, and kings in the brightness of your rising. Lift up your eyes round about, and see; they all gather together, they come to you; your sons shall come from far, and your daughters shall be carried in the arms. Then you shall see and be radiant, your heart

shall thrill and rejoice; because the abundance of the sea shall be turned to you, the wealth of the nations shall come to you. A multitude of camels shall cover you, the young camels of Midian and Ephah; all those from Sheba shall come. They shall bring gold and frankincense, and shall proclaim the praise of the Lord.
The word of the Lord.

RESPONSORIAL PSALM
Psalm 72:1-2.7-8.10-11.12-13 (R. cf. 11)
R. **All nations on earth shall fall prostrate before you, O Lord.**
O God, give your judgement to the king,
to a king's son your justice,
that he may judge your people injustice,
and your poor in right judgement. R.

In his days shall justice flourish,
and great peace till the moon is no more.
He shall rule from sea to sea,
from the River to the bounds of the earth. R.

The kings of Tarshish and the islands
shall pay him tribute.
The kings of Sheba and Seba

shall bring him gifts.
Before him all kings shall fall prostrate,
all nations shall serve him. R.

For he shall save the needy when they cry,
the poor, and those who are helpless.
He will have pity on the weak and the needy,
and save the lives of the needy. R.

SECOND READING Ephesians 3:2-3a.5-6
"It has now been revealed that the Gentiles are fellow heirs of the promise."
Brethren: I assume that you have heard of the stewardship of God's grace that was given to me for you, how the mystery was made known to me by revelation, which was not made known to the sons of men in other generations as it has now been revealed to his holy apostles and prophets by the Spirit; that is, how the Gentiles are fellow heirs, members of the same body, and partakers of the promise in Christ Jesus through the Gospel.
The word of the Lord.

Gospel Acclamation: Matthew 2:2
V. Alleluia. **R.** Alleluia. V. We have seen his star in the east, and have come to worship the Lord. **R.**

Alleluia.

GOSPEL Matthew 2:1-12

"We have come from the East to worship the king." Now when Jesus was born in Bethlehem of Judea in the days of Herod the king, behold, Wise Men from the East came to Jerusalem, saying, "Where is he who has been born king of the Jews? For we have seen his star in the East, and have come to worship him." When Herod the king heard this, he was troubled, and all Jerusalem with him; and assembling all the chief priests and scribes of the people, he inquired of them where the Christ was to be born. They told him, "In Bethlehem of Judea; for so it is written by the prophet: 'And you, O Bethlehem, in the land of Judah, are by no means least among the rulers of Judah; for from you shall come a ruler who will govern my people Israel.'" Then Herod summoned the Wise Men secretly and ascertained from them what time the star appeared; and he sent them to Bethlehem, saying, "Go and search diligently for the child, and when you have found him bring me word, that I too may come and worship him." When they had heard the king they went their way; and behold, the star which they had seen in the East went before them, till it came to rest over the place where the

child was. When they saw the star, they rejoiced exceedingly with great joy; and going into the house they saw the child with Mary his mother, and they fell down and worshipped him. Then, opening their treasures, they offered him gifts, gold and frankincense and myrrh. And being warned in a dream not to return to Herod, they departed to their own country by another way.

The Gospel of the Lord

January 6

You are Greater than those in the World

Daily Bread

Child of God, today you are about to discover your true identity. Before now people may be looking down at you. They may be taking you for granted but from now henceforth your true identity will be revealed!

The first thing you must know about yourself is that you are divinely connected. As one who is divinely connected whatever you ask God you will surely receive. As 1 John 3:22 declares, "Beloved: We receive from God whatever we ask, because we keep his commandments and do what pleases him." As long as you are ready to keep God's commandment, you will never lack! You will surely receive whatever you ask from God.

Child of God, do not allow anybody to deceive you! As St. John rightly declare, "Beloved, do not believe every spirit, but test the spirits to see whether they are of God; for many false prophets have gone out into the world. By this you know the Spirit of God: every spirit which confesses that Jesus Christ has come in the flesh is of God, and every spirit which does not confess Jesus is not of God. This is the spirit of antichrist, of which you heard that it was coming, and now it is in the world already." Take note, they are already in the world. By their fruits you shall know them!

As for you, "You are of God, and have overcome them; for he who is in you is greater than he who is in the world." As long as the One that is in you is greater, you are also great! Don't reduce yourself and don't allow anybody to reduce you. As you remain connected to our Lord Jesus Christ you will remain great and it shall be well with you in Jesus name – Amen!

St. Andre Bessette – Pray for Us!

Daily Readings:
MONDAY AFTER EPIPHANY

FIRST READING   1 John 3:22—1:6
"Test the spirits to see whether they are of God."

Beloved: We receive from God whatever we ask, because we keep his commandments and do what pleases him. And this is his commandment, that we should believe in the name of his Son Jesus Christ and love one another, just as he has commanded us. All who keep his commandments abide in him, and he in them. And by this we know that he abides in us, by the Spirit which he has given us. Beloved, do not believe every spirit, but test the spirits to see whether they are of God; for many false prophets have gone out into the world. By this you know the Spirit of God: every spirit which confesses that Jesus Christ has come in the flesh is of God, and every spirit which does not confess Jesus is not of God. This is the spirit of antichrist, of which you heard that it was coming, and now it is in the world already. Little children, you are of God, and have overcome them; for he who is in you is greater than he who is in the world. They are of the world, therefore what they say is of the world, and the world listens to them. We are of God. Whoever knows God listens to us, and he who is not of God does not listen to us. By this we know the spirit of truth and the spirit of error.

The word of the Lord

RESPONSORIAL PSALM

Psalm 2:7-8, 10-11 (R. 8a)

R. I will give you the nations as your inheritance.
I will announce the decree of the Lord:
The Lord said to me, "You are my Son.
It is I who have begotten you this day.
Ask of me and I will give you
the nations as your inheritance,
and the ends of the earth as your possession." R

"So now, O kings, understand;
take warning, rulers of the earth.
Serve the Lord with fear;
exult with trembling, pay him your homage." R

Gospel Acclamation: Matthew 4:23
V. Alleluia. R. Alleluia. V. Jesus was preaching the Gospel of the kingdom and healing every infirmity among the people. **V. Alleluia.**

GOSPEL   Matthew 4:12-17, 23-25
"The kingdom of heaven is at hand."
At that time: When Jesus heard that John had been arrested, he withdrew into Galilee; and leaving Nazareth he went and dwelt in Capernaum by the sea, in the territory of Zebulun and Naphtali, that

what was spoken by the prophet Isaiah might be fulfilled: "The land of Zebulun and the land of Naphtali. toward the sea, across the Jordan, Galilee of the Gentiles the people who sat in darkness have seen a great light, and for those who sat in the region and shadow of death light has dawned." From that time Jesus began to preach, saying, "Repent, for the kingdom of heaven is at hand." And he went about all Galilee, teaching in their synagogues and preaching the gospel of the kingdom and healing every disease and every infirmity among the people. So his fame spread throughout all Syria, and they brought him all the sick, those afflicted with various diseases and pains, demoniacs, epileptics, and paralytics, and he healed them. And great crowds followed him from Galilee and the Decapolis and Jerusalem and Judea and from beyond the Jordan.
The Gospel of the Lord

January 7
You are a Channel of Love

Daily Bread

Children of God are known by their love. Love is what unites and defines the followers of Christ. By their love you shall know them. Hatred is not for the children of God.

Child of God, as for you, you are a channel of love. 1 John 4:7-10 declares, "Beloved, let us love one another; for love is of God, and he who loves is born of God and knows God. He who does not love does not know God; for God is love." Love is the essence of God. Love is the best definition of God. In God we have our Loving Father, our Beloved Saviour, Jesus Christ and Holy Spirit, the Love that unites the Father, the Son and the rest of us.

In this the love of God was made manifest among us, that God sent his only-begotten Son into the world, so that we might live through him. In this is love, not that we loved God but that he loved us and sent his Son to be the expiation for our sins.

Child of God, as a channel of Love you will live through our Lord Jesus Christ. Through Him your sins will be forgiven. You will experience God's love and it shall be well with you in Jesus name – Amen!

St. Raymond of Penyafort – Pray for Us!

Daily Readings:
TUESDAY AFTER EPIPHANY

FIRST READING   1 John 4 7-10

"God is Love."

Beloved, let us love one another; for love is of God, and he who loves is born of God and knows God. He who does not love does not know God; for God is love. In this the love of God was made manifest among us, that God sent his only-begotten Son into the world, so that we might live through him. In this is love, not that we loved God but that he loved us and sent his Son to be the expiation for our sins.

The Gospel of the Lord

RESPONSORIAL PSALM

Psalm 72:1-2,3-4ab, 7-8 (R. see 11)

R. All nations on earth shall fall prostrate before you, O Lord.
O God, give your judgement to the king,
to a king's son your justice,
that he may judge your people in justice,
and your poor in right judgement.

May the mountains bring forth peace for the people,
and the hills justice.
May he defend the poor of the people,
and save the children of the needy. R

In his days shall justice flourish,
and great peace till the moon is no more.
He shall rule from sea to sea,
from the River to the bounds of the earth. R

Gospel Acclamation: Luke 4:18
V. Alleluia. R. Alleluia.
V. The Lord has sent me to preach good news to the poor, to proclaim release to the captives. **R. Alleluia.**

GOSPEL Mark 6:34-44
When Jesus multiplied the loaves, he showed himself as a prophet

At that time: Jesus saw a great throng, and he had compassion on them, because they were like sheep without a shepherd; and he began to teach them many things. And when it grew late, his disciples came to him and said, "This is a lonely place, and the hour is now late; send them away, to go into the country and villages round about and buy themselves something to eat." But he answered them, "You give them something to eat." And they said to him, "Shall we go and buy two hundred denarii worth of bread, and give it to them to eat?" And he said to them, "How many loaves have you? Go and see" And when they had found out, they said, "Five, and two fish." Then he commanded them all to sit down by companies upon the green grass. So they sat down in groups, by hundreds and by fifties. And taking the five loaves and the two fish he looked up to heaven, and blessed, and broke the loaves, and gave them to the disciples to set before the people; and he divided the two fish among them all. And they all ate and were satisfied. And they took up twelve baskets full of broken pieces and of the fish. And those who ate the loaves were five thousand men.

The Gospel of the Lord

January 8
God Abides in You!

Daily Bread

Child of God, do you know that you are not alone? And you will never be alone. God loves you! He not only loves you He abides in you!

As 1 John 4:11-18 rightly declares, "Beloved, if God so loved us, we also ought to love one another. No man has ever seen God; if we love one another, God abides in us and his love is perfected in us." As long as you love your fellow human being God will surely abide in you.

How then do you know when God abides in you? St. John declares, "By this we know that we abide in him and he in us, because he has given us of his own Spirit. And we have seen and testify that the Father has sent his Son as the Saviour of the world. Whoever confesses that Jesus is the Son of God, God abides in him, and he in God. So we know and believe the love God has for us. God is love, and he who abides in love abides in God, and God abides in him."

Do you know what happens when God abides in

you? In the gospel of John 15:5 our Lord Jesus Christ declares, "I am the vine, you *are* the branches. He who abides in Me, and I in him, bears much fruit." Child of God, as God abides in you, you will bear much fruit. Anything you lay your hands shall prosper. And it shall be well with you in Jesus name – Amen!

St. Severin of Noricum – Pray for Us!

Daily Readings:
WEDNESDAY AFTER EPIPHANY

FIRST READING   1 John 4:11-18
"If we love one another, God abides in us."
Beloved, if God so loved us, we also ought to love one another. No man has ever seen God; if we love one another, God abides in us and his love is perfected in us. By this we know that we abide in him and he in us, because he has given us of his own Spirit. And we have seen and testify that the Father has sent his Son as the Saviour of the world. Whoever confesses that Jesus is the Son of God, God abides in him, and he in God. So we know and believe the love God has for us. God is love, and he who abides in love abides in God, and God abides in him. In this is

love perfected with us, that we may have confidence for the day of judgement, because as he is so are we in this world. There is no fear in love, but perfect love casts out fear. For fear has to do with punishment, and he who fears is not perfected in love.

RESPONSORIAL PSALM
Psalm 72:1-2, 10-11, 12-13 (R. see 11)

R. All nations on earth shall fall prostrate before you, O Lord

O God, give your judgement to the king,
to a king's son your justice,
that he may judge your people in justice,
and your poor in right judgement. R

The kings of Tarshish and the islands
shall pay him tribute.
The kings of Sheba and Seba
shall bring him gifts.
Before him all kings shall fall prostrate,
all nations shall serve him. R

For he shall save the needy when they cry,
the poor, and those who are helpless.
He will have pity on the weak and the needy,
and save the lives of the needy. R

ALLELUIA — See 1 Timothy 3:16

V. Alleluia. R. Alleluia. V. Glory to you, O Christ, preached among the nations; glory to you, O Christ, believed on in the world. **R. Alleluia.**

GOSPEL — Mark 6:45-52

They saw him walking on the sea.
[After the five thousand men were satisfied,] Jesus immediately made his disciples get into the boat and go before him to the other side, to Bethsaida, while he dismissed the crowd. And after he had taken leave of them, he went up on the mountain to pray. And when evening came, the boat was out on the sea, and he was alone on the land. And he saw that they were distressed in rowing, for the wind was against them. And about the fourth watch of the night he came to them, walking on the sea. He meant to pass by them, but when they saw him walking on the sea they thought it was a ghost, and cried out; for they all saw him, and were terrified. But immediately he spoke to them and said, "Take heart, it is I; have no fear." And he got into the boat with them and the wind ceased. And they were utterly astounded, for they did not understand about the loaves, but their hearts were hardened.
The Gospel of the Lord

January 9

Hatred is Over!

Daily Bread

Hatred is worst than virus. It is the worst thing that can happen to any home. Where there is hatred there is no love and where there is no love there is strife, conflicts and all kinds of evil and wickedness. Love is the only way forward!

1 John 4:19 declares, "Beloved: We love God, because he first loved us. If anyone says, "I love God" and hates his brother, he is a liar; for he who does not love his brother whom he has seen, cannot love God whom he has not seen. And this commandment we have from him, that he who loves God should love his brother also."

With this declaration every spirit of hatred is cancelled! The yoke of hatred is broken. No more hatred! Those who hate you will start loving you. Your love is hereby restored in the name of God the Father, Son and Holy Spirit – Amen!

For this is the love of God, that we keep his commandments. And his commandments are not burdensome. For whatever is born of God overcomes the world; and this is the victory that overcomes the world, our faith. Child of God, as you love God and obey His commandments you will surely overcome the world and it shall be well with you in Jesus name – Amen!

St. Adrian of Canterbury – Pray for Us!

Daily Readings:
THURSDAY AFTER EPIPHANY

FIRST READING   **1 John 4:19—5:4**

"He who loves God should love his brother also."
Beloved: We love God, because he first loved us. If anyone says, "I love God" and hates his brother, he is a liar; for he who does not love his brother whom he has seen, cannot love God whom he has not seen. And this commandment we have from him, that he who loves God should love his brother also. Ever one who believes that Jesus is the Christ has been born of God, and everyone who loves the parent loves the one begotten by him. By this we know that we love the children of God, when we love God and obey his commandments. For this is the love of God, that we keep his commandments. And his commandments are not burdensome. For whatever is born of God

overcomes the world; and this is the victory that overcomes the world, our faith.
The word of the Lord

RESPONSORIAL PSALM
Psalm 72:1-2, 14   and   15cd, 17 (R.see 11)
R. All nations on earth shall fall prostrate before you, O Lord.
O God, give your judgement to the king,
to a king's son your justice,
that he may judge your people in justice,
and your poor in right judgement. R

From oppression and violence, he redeems their souls;
to him their blood is dear.
They shall pray for him without ceasing,
and bless him all the day. R

May his name endure for ever,
his name continue like the sun.
Every tribe shall be blest in him,
all nations shall call him blessed. R

Gospel Acclamation: Luke 4:18
V. Alleluia. **R.** Alleluia. **V.** The Lord has sent me to preach good news to the poor, to proclaim release to

the captives. **R.** Alleluia.

GOSPEL   **Luke 4:14-22a**

"Today this Scripture has been fulfilled."
At that time: Jesus returned in the power of the Spirit into Galilee, and a report concerning him went out through all the surrounding country. And he taught in their synagogues, being glorified by all. And he came to Nazareth, where he had been brought up; and he went to the synagogue, as was his custom, on the Sabbath day. And he stood up to read; and there was given to him the Book of the Prophet Isaiah. He opened the book and found the place where it was written, "The Spirit of the Lord is upon me, because he has anointed me to preach good news to the poor. He has sent me to proclaim release to the captives and recovering of sight to the blind, to set at liberty those who are oppressed, to proclaim the acceptable year of the Lord." And he closed the book, and gave it back to the attendant, and sat down; and the eyes of all in the synagogue were fixed on him. And he began to say to them, "Today this Scripture has been fulfilled in your hearing." And all spoke well of him, and wondered at the gracious words which proceeded out of his mouth.
The Gospel of the Lord

January 10

You are Destined for Eternal Life

Daily Bread

Eternal life is the reward of righteousness and uprightness. It is the reward that awaits God's children. Eternal damnation, on the other hand, is the punishment that awaits the sinners. Child of God, you are destined for eternal life.

1 John 5:5-13 declares, "Beloved: Who is it that overcomes the world but he who believes that Jesus is the Son of God? This is he who came by water and blood, Jesus Christ, not with the water only but with the water and the blood. And the Spirit is the witness, because the Spirit is the truth." Child of God, as long as you believe in Christ Jesus you are an overcomer.

There are three witnesses, the Spirit, the water, and the blood; and these three agree… He who does not believe God has made him a liar, because he has not believed in the testimony that God has borne to his Son. And this is the testimony that God gave us eternal life, and this life is in his Son. Child of God, the Lord God has given us Eternal Life through Son our Lord Jesus Christ!

"He who has the Son has life; he who has not the Son of God has no life. I write this to you who believe in the name of the Son of God, that you may know that you have eternal life." As long as you have God's Son, our Lord Jesus Christ, you will surely have eternal life and it shall be well with you in Jesus name – Amen!

St. Agatho Thaumaturgus – Pray for Us!

Daily Readings:
FRIDAY AFTER EPIPHANY

FIRST READING **1 John 5:5-13**

"The Spirit, the water, and the blood."
Beloved: Who is it that overcomes the world but he who believes that Jesus is the Son of God? This is he who came by water and blood, Jesus Christ, not with the water only but with the water and the blood. And the Spirit is the witness, because the Spirit is the truth. There are three witnesses, the Spirit, the water, and the blood; and these three agree. If we receive

the testimony of men, the testimony of God is greater; for this is the testimony of God that he has borne witness to his Son. He who believes in the Son of God has the testimony in himself. He who does not believe God has made him a liar, because he has not believed in the testimony that God has borne to his Son. And this is the testimony, that God gave us eternal life, and this life is in his Son. He who has the Son has life; he who has not the Son of God has not life. I write this to you who believe in the name of the Son of God, that you may know that you have eternal life. *The word of the Lord*

RESPONSORIAL PSALM
Psalm 147:12-13,14-15, 19-20 (R. 12a)
R. O Jerusalem, glorify the Lord!
O Jerusalem, glorify the **Lord!**
O Sion, praise your God!
He has strengthened the bars of your gates;
he has blessed your children within you. **R**

He established peace on your borders;
he gives you your fill of finest wheat.
He sends out his word to the earth,
and swiftly runs his command. **R**

He reveals his word to Jacob;
to Israel, his decrees and judgements.
He has not dealt thus with other nations;
he has not taught them his judgements. **R**

Gospel Acclamation: Matthew 4:23
V. **Alleluia. R. Alleluia. V.** Jesus was preaching the Gospel of the kingdom and healing every infirmity among the people. **R. Alleluia.**

GOSPEL Luke 5:12-16
"And immediately the leprosy left him."
While Jesus was in one of the cities, there came a man full of leprosy; and when he saw Jesus, he fell on his face and begged him, "Lord, if you will, you can make me clean." And he stretched out his hand, and touched him, saying, "I will; be clean." And immediately the leprosy left him. And he charged him to tell no one; but "go and show yourself to the priest, and make an offering for your cleansing, as Moses commanded, for a proof to the people." But so much the more the report went abroad concerning him; and great multitudes gathered to hear and to be healed of their infirmities. But he withdrew to the wilderness and prayed.
The Gospel of the Lord

January 11
Whatever You Ask You Shall Receive

Daily Bread

Who says your prayer cannot be answered? Who says you will not receive that which you have been asking for? And who says God will not grant your heart desire any moment from now? Worry not! Your period of waiting is over! God is about to answer your prayers!

First John 5:14-21 declares, "Beloved: This is the confidence which we have in the Son of God, that if we ask anything according to his will he hears us. If we know that he hears us in whatever we ask, we know that we have obtained the requests made of him." Child of God, as long as you pray in accordance to God's will, God will surely answer your prayer.

In Luke 22:42 our Lord Jesus Christ prayed, saying, "Father, if it is Your will, take this cup away from Me; nevertheless not My will, but Yours, be done." God answered his prayer in accordance to His will. He did not take away the cup of suffering. He allowed Him to drink the cup of suffering but after three days; God raised him and gave him the name that is above every other name (Philippians 2:9-10). God's will for him was the best! Indeed, God answers all prayers not necessarily the way we want it but in accordance to His will.

No wonder our Lord Jesus Christ declares in Matthew 7:7-11 Ask, and it will be given to you; seek, and you will find; knock, and it will be opened to you. For everyone who asks receives, and he who seeks finds, and to him who knocks it will be opened. Or what man is there among you who, if his son asks for bread, will give him a stone? Or if he asks for a fish, will he give him a serpent? If you then, being evil, know how to give good gifts to your children, how much more will your Father who is in heaven give good things to those who ask Him!

In John 15:7 our Lord Jesus Christ assures his followers: "If you abide in Me, and My words abide in you, you will ask what you desire, and it shall be done for you. By this My Father is glorified, that you bear much fruit; so you will be My disciple." As you continue to abide in God through our Lord Jesus

Christ, there is nothing you ask that you will not receive.

In John 16:23-24 Jesus insisted, "Most assuredly, I say to you, whatever you ask the Father in My name He will give you. Until now you have asked nothing in My name. Ask, and you will receive, that your joy may be full." This is exactly what open cheque is all about! Child of God, the ball is in your court. Don't ever get tired of praying. As you pray God will surely answer your prayer and you will experience fullness of joy!

You may be wondering why so many people's prayers are not answered. James 4:3 has an answer to this perennial question. "You ask and do not receive, because you ask amiss, that you may spend *it* on your pleasures." Most people pray wrongly and that is why their prayers are not answered.

Finally, as St. Paul rightly declares in his letter to the Philippians 4:6-7, "Be anxious for nothing, but in everything by prayer and supplication, with thanksgiving, let your requests be made known to God; and the peace of God, which surpasses all understanding, will guard your hearts and minds through Christ Jesus our Lord – Amen!

St. Theodosius of Cenobiarch – Pray for Us!

Daily Readings:
SATURDAY AFTER EPIPHANY

FIRST READING   1 John 5:14-2

"He hears us in whatever we ask."

Beloved: This is the confidence which we have in the Son of God, that if we ask anything according to his will he hears us. And if we know that he hears us in whatever we ask, we know that we have obtained the requests made of him. If any one sees his brother committing what is not a deadly sin, he will ask, and God will give him life for those whose sin is not deadly. There is sin which is deadly; I do not say that one is to pray for that. All wrongdoing is sin, but there is sin which is not deadly. We know that any one born of God does not sin, but He who was born of God keeps him, and the Evil One does not touch him. We know that we are of God, and the whole world is in the power of the Evil One. And we know that the Son of God has come and has given us understanding, to know him who is true; and we are in him who is true, in his Son Jesus Christ. This is the true God and eternal life. Little children, keep yourselves from idols. **The word of the Lord**

RESPONSORIAL PSALM
Psalm 149:1b-2, 3-4, 5-6a and 9bc (R. 4a)
R. The Lord takes delight in his people.
Sing a new song to the **Lord**,
his praise in the assembly of the faithful.
Let Israel rejoice in its Maker;
let Sion's children exult in their king. **R**

Let them praise his name with dancing,
and make music with timbrel and harp.
For the **Lord** takes delight in his people;
he crowns the poor with salvation. **R**

Let the faithful exult in glory,
and rejoice as they take their rest.
Let the praise of God be in their mouths.
This is an honour for all his faithful. **R**

ALLELUIA   Matthew 4:16
V. Alleluia. Alleluia. **V.** The people who sat in darkness have seen a great light, and for those who sat in the region and shadow of death light has dawned. **R.** Alleluia.

GOSPEL   John 3:22-30
"The friend of the bridegroom rejoices greatly at the

bridegroom's voice."

At that time: Jesus and his disciples went into the land of Judea; there he remained with them and baptised. John also was baptizing at Aenon near Salim, because there was much water there; and people came and were baptised. For John had not yet been put in prison. Now a discussion arose between John's disciples and a Jew over purifying. And they came to John, and said to him, "Rabbi, he who was with you beyond the Jordan, to whom you bore witness, here he is, baptizing, and all are going to him." John answered, "No one can receive anything except what is given him from heaven. You yourselves bear me witness, that I said, I am not the Christ, but I have been sent before him. He who has the bride is the bridegroom; the friend of the bridegroom, who stands and hears him, rejoices greatly at the bridegroom's voice; therefore, this joy of mine is now full. He must increase, but I must decrease."

The Gospel of the Lord

January 12
Baptism of Divine Consolation

Daily Bread

Our Lord Jesus Christ has come to console His people through baptism. Today happens to be the Baptism of our Lord Jesus Christ. Catechism of the Catholic Church paragraph 1277 defines baptism as a new birth in Christ, "Baptism is birth into the new life in Christ. In accordance with the Lord's will, it is necessary for salvation, as is the Church herself, which we enter by Baptism." Baptism is indeed necessary for our salvation!

This is exactly what our Lord Jesus meant when He said in John 3:5 "Truly, I say to you, unless one is born of water and the Spirit, he cannot enter the kingdom of God." Baptism is a channel of God's Kingdom.

The gospel of Luke 3:15-22 presents the baptism of our Lord Jesus Christ. John told his fellow Jews, "I baptise you with water; but he who is mightier than

I is coming, the thong of whose sandals I am not worthy to untie; he will baptise you with the Holy Spirit and with fire." Baptism of the Holy Spirit is the baptism of Divine Consolation. Hence, the Holy Spirit is our Comforter!

Something remarkable happened during the baptism of our Lord Jesus Christ, "When all the people were baptised, and when Jesus also had been baptised and was praying, the heaven was opened, and the Holy Spirit descended upon him in bodily form, as a dove, and a voice came from heaven, "You are my beloved Son; with you I am well pleased." This is one of the Comforting statements in the bible. God the Father came not just to introduce His beloved Son but also to bring consolation to His children through our Lord Jesus Christ.

This baptism of Divine consolation is made clearly in Isaiah 40:1-11 where the Lord God says, "Comfort, comfort my people, says your God. Speak tenderly to Jerusalem, and cry to her that her warfare is ended, that her iniquity is pardoned..."

Child of God, the Lord God has come to comfort you! He has come to wipe away all your tears and sinfulness with the water of baptism. He is your Comforter. He has come to console you. He has come to reward you.

As Isaiah 4:9-11 declares "Behold your God!" Behold, the Lord God comes with might, and his arm rules for him; behold, his reward is with him, and his recompense before him. He will feed his flock like a shepherd, he will gather the lambs in his arms, He will carry them in his bosom, and gently lead those that are with young.

In his letter to Titus 2:11-14, St. Paul sums up other benefits of baptism: "Beloved: For the grace of God has appeared for the salvation of all men, training us to renounce irreligion and worldly passions, and to live sober, upright, and godly lives in this world… when the goodness and loving kindness of God our Saviour appeared, he saved us, not because of deeds done by us in righteousness, but in virtue of his own mercy, by the washing of regeneration and renewal in the Holy Spirit, which he poured out upon us richly through Jesus Christ our Saviour, so that we might be justified by his grace and become heirs in hope of eternal life.

Baptism therefore is for the salvation of all men, for the washing of regeneration, for the renewal in the Holy Spirit, for our justification and inheritance as coheirs of Christ.

Child of God, as you renew your baptismal promises may God cleanse you and grant you His Salvation and justification in Jesus name – Amen!

Happy Baptism of the LORD!

Daily Readings:
BAPTISM OF THE LORD

Entrance Antiphon   Cf. Mt 3:16-17
After the Lord was baptised, the heavens were opened, and the Spirit descended upon him like a dove, and the voice of the Father thundered: This is my beloved Son, in whom I am well pleased.

Collect
Almighty ever-living God, who, when Christ had been baptised in the River Jordan, and as the Holy Spirit descended upon him, solemnly declared him your beloved Son, grant that your children by adoption, reborn of water and the Holy Spirit, may always be well pleasing to you.
Through our Lord Jesus Christ, your Son, who lives and reigns with you in the unity of the Holy Spirit, one God, for ever and ever

FIRST READING Isaiah 40:1-5.9-11

"The glory of the Lord shall be revealed, and all flesh shall see it together."

Comfort, comfort my people, says your God. Speak tenderly to Jerusalem, and cry to her that her warfare is ended, that her iniquity is pardoned, that she has received from the Lord's hand double for all her sins. A voice cries: "In the wilderness prepare the way of the Lord, make straight in the desert a highway for our God. Every valley shall be lifted up, and every mountain and hill be made low; the uneven ground shall become level, and the rough places a plain. And the glory of the Lord shall be revealed, and all flesh shall see it together, for the mouth of the Lord has spoken." Get you up to a high mountain, O Zion, herald of good tidings; lift up your voice with strength, O Jerusalem, herald of good tidings, lift it up, fear not; say to the cities of Judah, "Behold your God!" Behold, the Lord God comes with might, and his arm rules for him; behold, his reward is with him, and his recompense before him. He will feed his flock like a shepherd, he will gather the lambs in his arms, he will carry them in his bosom, and gently lead those that are with young.

The word of the Lord.

RESPONSORIAL PSALM
Psalm 104: 1b-2.3-4.24-25.27-28.29-30 (R. 1)

R. Bless the Lord, O my soul!
  O Lord my God, you are very great!
O Lord my God, how great you are,
clothed in majesty and honour,
wrapped in light as with a robe!
You stretch out the heavens like a tent. R.

On the waters you establish your dwelling.
You make the clouds your chariot;
you ride on the wings of the wind.
You make the winds your messengers,
flame and fire your servants. R.

How many are your works, O Lord!
In wisdom you have made them all.
The earth is full of your creatures.
Vast and wide is the span of the sea,
with its creeping things past counting,
living things great and small. R.

All of these look to you
to give them their food in due season.
You give it, they gather it up;
you open wide your hand, they are well filled. R.

You hide your face, they are dismayed;
you take away their breath, they die,
returning to the dust from which they came.
You send forth your spirit, and they are created,
and you renew the face of the earth. R.

SECOND READING   Titus 2:11-14;   3:4-7
"He saved us by the washing of regeneration and renewal in the Holy Spirit."

Beloved: For the grace of God has appeared for the salvation of all men, training us to renounce irreligion and worldly passions, and to live sober, upright, and godly lives in this world, awaiting our blessed hope, the appearing of the glory of our great God and Saviour Jesus Christ, who gave himself for us to redeem us from all iniquity and to purify for himself a people of his own who are zealous for good deeds. But when the goodness and loving kindness of God our Saviour appeared, he saved us, not because of deeds done by us in righteousness, but in virtue of his own mercy, by the washing of regeneration and renewal in the Holy Spirit, which he poured out upon us richly through Jesus Christ our Saviour, so that we might be justified by his grace and become heirs in hope of eternal life.
The word of the Lord.

Gospel Acclamation: Cf. Luke 3:16
V. **Alleluia. R. Alleluia.** V. John said: He who is coming is mightier than I; he will baptise you with the Holy Spirit and with fire **R.** Alleluia.

GOSPEL Luke 3:15-16.21-22
"When Jesus had been baptised and was praying, the heaven was opened."
At that time: As the people were in expectation, and all men questioned in their hearts concerning John, whether perhaps he were the Christ, John answered them all, "I baptise you with water; but he who is mightier than I is coming, the thong of whose sandals I am not worthy to untie; he will baptise you with the Holy Spirit and with fire." Now when all the people were baptised, and when Jesus also had been baptised and was praying, the heaven was opened, and the Holy Spirit descended upon him in bodily form, as a dove, and a voice came from heaven, "You are my beloved Son; with you I am well pleased." *The Gospel of the Lord.*

Prayer over the Offerings
Accept, O Lord, the offerings we have brought to honour the revealing of your beloved Son, so that the oblation of your faithful may be transformed into the

sacrifice of him, who willed in his compassion to wash away the sins of the world. Who lives and reigns for ever and ever.

Communion Antiphon Jn 1:32.34
Behold the One of whom John said:
I have seen and testified that this is the Son of God.

Prayer after Communion
Nourished with these sacred gifts, we humbly entreat your mercy, O Lord, that, faithfully listening to your Only Begotten Son, we may be your children in name and in truth. Through Christ our Lord.

JANUARY 13

YOU NOW HAVE A DIRECT ACCESS TO GOD

Daily Bread

Gone were the days when you needed a prophet or a visionary before you could get access to God. Gone were the days when God was so far away from his children that nobody could even hear His voice and live. Today, the barrier that is separating you from God has been broken!

Hebrew 1:1-6 declares, "In many and various ways God spoke of old to our fathers by the prophets; but in these last days he has spoken to us by a Son, whom he appointed the heir of all things, through whom also he created the ages. He reflects the glory of God and bears the very stamp of his nature.

Child of God, you don't need any prophet before you could hear from God. All you need is Jesus Christ. As Jesus rightly declares in John 14:6, "I am the way, the truth, and the life. No one comes to the Father except through Me." Through our Lord Jesus Christ you will have direct access to God. Your vision and your prophetic gifs will be restored. You will hear from God and God will hear from you. And it shall be well with you in Jesus name – Amen!

St. Hilary – Pray for Us!

Daily Readings:
MONDAY OF FIRST WEEK IN ORDINARY TIME

FIRST READING   Hebrews 1:1-6
"He has spoken to us by a Son."
In many and various ways God spoke of old to our fathers by the prophets; but in these last days he has spoken to us by a Son, whom he appointed the heir of all things, through whom also he created the ages. He reflects the glory of God and bears the very stamp of his nature, upholding the universe by his word of power. When he had made purification for sins, he sat down at the right hand of the Majesty on high, having become as much superior to angels as the name he has obtained is more excellent than theirs. For to what angel did God ever say, "You are my Son, today I have begotten you"? Or again, "I will be to him a father, and he shall be to me a son"? And

again, when he brings the first-born into the world, he says, "Let all God's angels worship him."
The word of the Lord.

RESPONSORIAL PSALM
Psalm 97:1 and 2b, 6 and 7c, 9 (R. see 7c)
R/ Worship God, all you angels
The **Lord** is king, let earth rejoice;
let the many islands be glad.
Justice and right are the foundation of his throne. R

The skies proclaim his justice;
all peoples see his glory.
All you angels, worship him. R

For you indeed are the **Lord**
most high above all the earth,
exalted far above all gods. **R**

Gospel Acclamation: Mark 1:15
V/Alleluia. R/. Alleluia. V/The kingdom of God is at hand; repent, and believe in the Gospel. **R/ Alleluia**

GOSPEL   Mark 1:14-20
"Repent, and believe in the Gospel."
After John was arrested, Jesus came into Galilee,

preaching the gospel of God, and saying, "The time is fulfilled, and the kingdom of God is at hand; repent, and believe in the gospel." And passing along by the Sea of Galilee, he saw Simon and Andrew the brother of Simon casting a net in the sea; for they were fishermen. And Jesus said to them, "Follow me and I will make you become fishers of men." And immediately they left their nets and followed him. And going on a little farther, he saw James the son of Zebedee and John his brother, who were in their boat mending the nets. And immediately he called them; and they left their father Zebedee in the boat with the hired servants, and followed him.

The Gospel of the Lord

January 14

You are Crowed with Glory and Honour

Daily Bread

Today is a day you will live to remember. You are about to discover your true identity. Before now you may be underrating yourself. You might have even seen yourself as good for nothing. But today, God has come to restore your lost glory!

Hebrews 2:5-12 declares, "It was not to angels that God subjected the world to come, of which we are speaking. It has been testified somewhere, "What is man that you are mindful of him, or the son of man, that you care for him? You made him for a little while lower than the angels, You have crowned him with glory and honour, putting everything in subjection under his feet."

Child of God, as you can see, God is mindful of you. He cares for you. He has made you higher than the angels. He has placed all things under your feet. And above all, He has crowned you with glory and honour. From today, you will celebrate and you will be celebrated. And it shall be well with you in Jesus name – Amen!

St. Felix of Nola – Pray for Us!

Daily Readings:
TUESDAY OF THE FIRST WEEK IN ORDINARY TIME

FIRST READING   **Hebrews 2:5-12**

"It was fitting that he should make the pioneer of their salvation perfect through suffering."

It was not to angels that God subjected the world to come, of which we are speaking. It has been testified somewhere, "What is man that you are mindful of him, or the son of man, that you care for him? You made him for a little while lower than the angels, You have crowned him with glory and honour, putting everything in subjection under his feet." Now in putting everything in subjection to him, he left nothing outside his control. As it is, we do not yet see everything in subjection to him. But we see Jesus, who for a little while was made lower than the angels, crowned with glory and honour because of the suffering of death, so that by the grace of God he might taste death for everyone. For it was fitting that he, for whom and by whom all things exist, in bringing many sons to glory, should make the pioneer of their salvation perfect through suffering. For he who sanctifies and those who are sanctified have all one origin. That is why he is not ashamed to call them brethren, saying, "I will proclaim your name to my brethren; in the midst of the congregation, I will praise you!" The word of the Lord

RESPONSORIAL PSALM
Psalm 8:2ab and 5, 6-7a, 7b-9 (R. see 7a)
R/ You have given your Son power over the works of your hands.
O Lord, our Lord, how majestic
is your name through all the earth!
What is man that you should keep him in mind,
the son of man that you care for him? R/

Yet you have made him little lower than the angels;
with glory and honour you crowned him,
gave him power over the works of your hands. R/

You put all things under his feet,
all of them, sheep and oxen,

yes, even the cattle of the fields,
birds of the air, and fish of the sea
that make their way through the waters.

Gospel Acclamation: 1 Thessalonians 2:13
V/. Alleluia R. Alleluia. V/Accept the word of God, not as the word of men, but as what it really is, the word of God. **R/ Alleluia.**

GOSPEL Mark 1:2 lb-28

"He taught them as one who had authority."
In the city of Capernaum, Jesus entered the synagogue on the sabbath and taught. And they were astonished at his teaching, for he taught them as one who had authority, and not as the scribes. And immediately there was in their synagogue a man with an unclean spirit; and he cried out, "What have you to do with us, Jesus of Nazareth? Have you come to destroy us? I know who you are, the Holy One of God." But Jesus rebuked him, saying, "Be silent, and come out of him!" And the unclean spirit, convulsing him and crying with a loud voice, came out of him.
And they were all amazed, so that they questioned among themselves, saying, "What is this? A new teaching! With authority he commands even the unclean spirits, and they obey him." And at once his

fame spread everywhere throughout all the surrounding region of Galilee.

The Gospel of the Lord

January 15
You Shall Be Delivered from Lifelong Bondage

Daily Bread

Child of God, your period of bondage and captivity is over! The Lord has come to deliver you from lifelong bondage. He has come to set you free. God has come to restore your lost glory. He has come to help you!

Hebrews 2:14-18 declares, "Since the children share in flesh and blood, Jesus himself likewise partook of the same nature, that through death he might destroy him who has the power of death, that is, the devil, and deliver all those who through fear of death were subject to lifelong bondage.

Through his death on the Cross of Calvary our Lord Jesus Christ has destroyed the devil and the forces of death. Child of God, death has no more power over you! You will not die untimely death! Premature death will never be your portion.

God has also come to deliver you from the spirit

of fear, especially the fear of death. As the Lord God rightly declares in Isaiah 43:1-3 "Fear not, for I have redeemed you; I have called *you* by your name; You *are* Mine. When you pass through the waters, I *will be* with you; And through the rivers, they shall not overflow you. When you walk through the fire, you shall not be burned, Nor shall the flame scorch you. For I *am* the Lord your God, The Holy One of Israel, your Savior." Child of God, you are hereby declared free from the spirit of fear and anxiety in the name of God the Father, God the Son and God the Holy Spirit – Amen! Your period of bondage is over! Rejoice and be glad for your case is settled!

St. Paul the First Hermit – Pray for Us!

Daily Readings:
WEDNESDAY OF THE FIRST WEEK IN ORDINARY TIME

FIRST READING   Hebrew 2:14-18
"He had to be made like his brethren in every respect, so that he might become merciful."
Since the children share in flesh and blood, Jesus himself likewise partook of the same nature, that

through death he might destroy him who has the power of death, that is, the devil, and deliver all those who through fear of death were subject to lifelong bondage. For surely it is not with angels that he is concerned but with the descendants of Abraham. Therefore he had to be made like his brethren in every respect, so that he might become a merciful and faithful high priest in the service of God, to make expiation for the sins of the people. For because he himself has suffered and been tempted, he is able to help those who are tempted.
The word of the Lord

RESPONSORIAL PSALM
Psalm 105:1-2, 3-4, 6-7,8-9 (R. 8a)
R./ The Lord remembers his covenant for ever.
Give thanks to the **Lord;** proclaim his name.
Make known his deeds among the peoples.
O sing to him, sing his praise;
tell all his wonderful works! **R/**

Glory in his holy name;
let the hearts that seek the Lord rejoice.
Turn to the **Lord** and his strength;
constantly seek his face. **R/**

O children of Abraham, his servant,
O descendants of the Jacob he chose,
he, the **Lord,** is our God;
his judgements are in all the earth. **R/**

He remembers his covenant for ever:
the promise he ordained for a thousand generations,
the covenant he made with Abraham,
the oath he swore to Isaac, **R/**

Gospel Acclamation: John 10:27
V/ **Alleluia. R/ Alleluia.** V/ My sheep hear my voice, says the Lord; and I know them, and they follow me. R/Alleluia.

GOSPEL   Mark 1:29-39
"He healed many who were sick with diseases."
At that time: Jesus left the synagogue, and entered the house of Simon and Andrew, with James and John. Now Simon's mother-in-law lay sick with a fever, and immediately they told him of her. And he came and took her by the hand and lifted her up, and the fever left her; and she served them. That evening, at sundown, they brought to him all who were sick or possessed with demons. And the whole city was gathered together about the door. And he healed

many who were sick with various diseases, and cast out many demons; and he would not permit the demons to speak, because they knew him. And in the morning, a great while before day, he rose and went out to a lonely place, and there he prayed. And Simon and those who were with him followed him, and they found him and said to him, "Every one is searching for you." And he said to them, "Let us go on to the next towns, that I may preach there also; for that is why I came out." And he went throughout all Galilee, preaching in their synagogues and casting out demons.

The Gospel of the Lord

JANUARY 16

YOU SHALL HEAR THE VOICE OF THE LORD

Daily Bread

Have you ever heard from God? Do you know what it means to hear from God? Have you ever tried to communicate with God directly? Today, your channel of divine communication is about to be restored!

Hebrews 3:7-14 declares, "Brethren: As the Holy Spirit says, "Today, when you hear his voice, do not harden your hearts as in the rebellion, on the day of testing in the wilderness, where your fathers put me to the test and saw my works for forty years.

In the gospel of Mark 7:34-35 a deaf and dumb man was brought to Jesus and Jesus "looking up to heaven, sighed, and said to him, "Ephphatha," that is, "Be opened." Immediately his ears were opened, and the [l]impediment of his tongue was loosed, and he spoke plainly."

Child of God, I may not know what is blocking

your ears from hearing directly from God, but right now I cast out whatever that blocking your ears. Receive your restoration. From today, as you hear from God you will no longer harden your hearts. You will hear directly from God and God will your voice whenever you pray to Him and it shall be well with you in Jesus name – Amen!

St. Joseph of Vaz – Pray for Us!

Daily Readings:
THURSDAY OF THE FIRST WEEK IN ORDINARY TIME

FIRST READING   Hebrews   3:7-14

"Exhort one another every day, as long as it is called 'today.'"

Brethren: As the Holy Spirit says, "Today, when you hear his voice, do not harden your hearts as in the rebellion, on the day of testing in the wilderness, where your fathers put me to the test and saw my works for forty years. Therefore, I was provoked with that generation, and said, 'They always go astray in their hearts; they have not known my ways.' As I swore in my wrath, 'They shall never enter my rest.'" Take care, brethren, lest there be in

any of you an evil, unbelieving heart, leading you to fall away from the living God. But exhort one another every day, as long as it is called "today," that none of you may be hardened by the deceitfulness of sin. For we share in Christ, if only we hold our first confidence firm to the end.
The word of the Lord

RESPONSORIAL PSALM
Psalm 95:6-7abc, 7d and 8-9, 10-11 (R. 8a)
R/ Harden not your hearts
O come; let us bow and bend low.
Let us kneel before the God who made us,
for he is our God and we
the people who belong to his pasture,
the flock that is led by his hand. **R/**

O that today you would listen to his voice!
"Harden not your hearts as at Meribah,
as on that day at Massah in the desert
when your forebears put me to the test;
when they tried me, though they saw my work." **R/**

"For forty years I wearied of that generation,
and I said, 'Their hearts are astray;
this people does not know my ways.'

Then I took an oath in my anger,
'Never shall they enter my rest.' **R/**

Gospel Acclamation: Matthew 4:23
V/ Alleluia. **R/** Alleluia. **V/** Jesus was preaching the Gospel of the kingdom and healing every infirmity among the people. **R/** Alleluia.

GOSPEL   Mark 1:40-45

"The leprosy left him, and he was made clean."
At that time: A leper came to Jesus begging him, and kneeling said to him, "If you will, you can make me clean." Moved with pity, he stretched out his hand and touched him, and said to him, "I will; be clean." And immediately the leprosy left him, and he was made clean. And he sternly charged him, and sent him away at once, and said to him, "See that you say nothing to any one; but go, show yourself to the priest, and offer for your cleansing what Moses commanded, for a proof to the people." But he went out and began to talk freely about it, and to spread the news, so that Jesus could no longer openly enter a town, but was out in the country; and people came to him from every quarter.
The Gospel of the Lord.

January 17
You shall Experience God's Rest

Daily Bread

Today, God has come to deliver you from anxiety and the spirit of restlessness. Your period of sleepless night is coming to an end! With this declaration you will not experience unnecessary worries again!

Hebrew 4:1-5, 11 declares, "Brethren: While the promise of entering his rest remains, let us fear lest any of you be judged to have failed to reach it." Child of God, you will surely reach your place of rest! Nothing and nobody can stop you from reaching your place of rest!

Right from time immemorial, God does not want you to break down that why He created night and the seventh day as a day of Rest. Hence, as the book of Hebrew 4 declares, "For he has somewhere spoken of the seventh day in this way, "And God rested on the seventh day from all his works." And again in this place he said, "They shall never enter my rest." Let us therefore strive to enter that rest that no one falls by the same sort of disobedience. So shall it be in Jesus name!

In the gospel of Matthew 11:28-29 our Lord Jesus Christ declares, "Come to Me, all *you* who labour and are heavy laden, and I will give you rest. Take My yoke upon you and learn from Me, for I am gentle and lowly in heart, and you will find rest for your souls." As you strive to enter God's place of rest you shall experience inner peace, inner joy and inner fulfilment. And it shall be well with you in Jesus name – Amen!

St. Anthony the Great – Pray for Us!

Daily Readings:
FRIDAY OF THE FIRST WEEK IN ORDINARY TIME

FIRST READING: Hebrews 4:1-5, 11

"Let us therefore strive to enter that rest."
Brethren: While the promise of entering his rest remains, let us fear lest any of you be judged to have failed to reach it. For good news came to us just as to them; but the message which they heard did not benefit them, because it did not meet with faith in the

hearers. For we who have believed enter that rest, as he has said, "As I swore in my wrath, 'They shall never enter my rest,'" although his works were finished from the foundation of the world. For he has somewhere spoken of the seventh day in this way, "And God rested on the seventh day from all his works." And again, in this place he said, "They shall never enter my rest." Let us therefore strive to enter that rest, that no one fall by the same sort of disobedience.

The word of the Lord.

RESPONSORIAL PSALM
Psalm 78:3 and 4bc, 6c-7, 8 (R. see 7b)
R/ **Never forget the deeds of God!**
The things we have heard and understood,
the things our fathers have told us,
but will tell them to the next generation:
the glories of the Lord and his might.

They should arise and declare it to their children,
that they should set their hope in God,
and never forget God's deeds,
but keep every one of his commands, R

So that they might not be like their fathers,
a defiant and rebellious generation,
a generation whose heart was fickle,
whose spirit was not faithful to God.

Gospel Acclamation: Luke 7:16
V/ Alleluia. R/Alleluia. V/ A great prophet has risen among us, and God has visited his people. R/ Alleluia.

GOSPEL   Mark 2:1-12
"The Son of man has authority on earth to forgive sins."

When Jesus returned to Capernaum after some days, it was reported that he was at home. And many were gathered together, so that there was no longer room for them, not even about the door; and he was preaching the word to them. And they came, bringing to him a paralytic carried by four men. And when they could not get near him because of the crowd, they removed the roof above him; and when they had made an opening, they let down the pallet on which the paralytic lay. And when Jesus saw their faith, he said to the paralytic, "Child, your sins are forgiven." Now some of the scribes were sitting there, questioning in their hearts, "Why does this man speak like this? It is blasphemy! Who can forgive sins but God alone?" And immediately Jesus, perceiving in his spirit that they questioned like this within themselves, said to them, "Why do you question like this in your hearts? Which is easier, to say to the paralytic, 'Your sins are forgiven,' or to say, 'Rise, take up your pallet and walk'? But that you may know that the Son of man has authority on earth to forgive sins" — he said to the paralytic— "I say to you, rise, take up your pallet and go home." And he rose, and immediately took up the pallet and went out before them all; so that they were all amazed and glorified God, saying, "We never saw anything like this!"

The Gospel of the Lord.

January 18

You Shall Receive Grace and Mercy

Daily Bread

If there is anything you need urgently, it is the grace of God. And if there is anything you cannot do without, it is the mercy of God. Grace is unmerited favour whereas mercy is God's tender love and compassion. Our God is a gracious God. He is also a Merciful Father.

In his letter to the Ephesians 2:8–9 St. Paul defines Grace as God's saving gift. "For by grace you have been saved through faith. And this is not your own doing; it is the gift of God, not a result of works."

The book of Lamentations 3:22-23 declares, The steadfast love of the LORD never ceases; his mercies never come to an end; they are new every morning; great is your faithfulness." God's merciful love is everlasting. His mercy does not come to an end.

Hebrews 4:15-16 noted, "For we have not a high priest who is unable to sympathize with our weaknesses, but one who in every respect has been tempted as we are, yet without sinning. Let us then with confidence draw near to the throne of grace, that we may receive mercy and find grace to help in time of need." As you draw near to the throne of grace you shall receive mercy and grace in Jesus name!

Our Lord Jesus Christ is not just a Merciful Lord He is also a Compassionate Saviour. He understands us and He sympathizes with our weakness. Psalm 130:3-4 raised a fundamental question, "If You, Lord, should mark iniquities, O Lord, who could stand? But there is forgiveness with You, That You may be feared." To sin is human but to forgive is Divine.

Mercy is among the essential attributes of God. In Exodus 34:6-7 the Lord God reveals His true identity, "The Lord, the Lord God, merciful and gracious, longsuffering, and abounding in goodness and truth, keeping mercy for thousands, forgiving iniquity and transgression and sin." Indeed, our God is a Merciful God. His Mercy endures forever.

Our God is not just merciful, for St. Paul He is also rich in mercy "But God, being rich in mercy, because of the great love with which he loved us, even when we were dead in our trespasses, made us alive together with Christ—by grace you have been saved—and raised us up with him and seated us with him in the heavenly places in Christ Jesus. **(Ephesians 2:4–6)**

In the gospel of Luke 6:36 our Lord Jesus Christ invites us to "Be merciful, just as your Father is merciful." And in the gospel of Matthew 5:7 He said in one his beatitudes, "Blessed *are* the merciful, for they shall obtain mercy." Child of God, if you want to obtain mercy from God then you must be merciful like God.

To crown it all in the gospel of **Matthew 9:13 our Lord Jesus Christ declares,** "Go and learn what this means: 'I desire mercy, and not sacrifice.' For I came not to call the righteous, but sinners." And in the Lord's Prayer our Lord Jesus Christ taught us how to obtain mercy from God. We are asked to pray, "Forgive us our debts, as we forgive our debtors." So, if you want God to forgive you then you must be ready to forgive your fellow human beings.

Finally, as the Psalmist declares, in Psalm 23:6 "Surely goodness and mercy shall follow us all the days of our lives, and we shall dwell in the house of the Lord forever and ever – Amen!

St. Emilie de Vialar – Pray for Us!

Daily Readings:
SATURDAY OF THE FIRST WEEK IN ORDINARY TIME

FIRST READING   **Hebrews 4:12-16**

"Let us then with confidence draw near to the throne of grace."

Brethren: The word of God is living and active, sharper than any two-edged sword, piercing to the division of soul and spirit, of joints and marrow, and discerning the thoughts and intentions of the heart. And before him no creature is hidden, but all are open and laid bare to the eyes of him with whom we have to do. Since then, we have a great high priest who has passed through the heavens, Jesus, the Son of God, let us hold fast our confession. For we have not a high priest who is unable to sympathize with our weaknesses, but one who in every respect has been tempted as we are, yet without sinning. Let us then with confidence draw near to the throne of grace, that we may receive mercy and find grace to help in time of need.

The word of the Lord.

RESPONSORIAL PSALM
Psalm 19:8, 9, 10, 15 (R.see John 6:63c)
R/Your words, O Lord, are Spirit and life.

The law of the Lord is perfect;
it revives the soul.
The decrees of the Lord are steadfast;
they give wisdom to the simple. R

The precepts of the Lord are right;
they gladden the heart.
The command of the Lord is clear;
it gives light to the eyes. R

The fear of the Lord is pure,
abiding for ever.
The judgements of the Lord are true;
they are, all of them, just. R

May the spoken words of my mouth,
the thoughts of my heart,
win favour in your sight, O Lord,
my rock and my redeemer!

Gospel Acclamation: Luke 4:18
V. Alleluia. V/Alleluia. *V.* The Lord has sent me to

preach good news to the poor, to proclaim release to the captives. Alleluia.

GOSPEL   Mark 2:13-17

"I came not to call the righteous, but sinners." At that time: Jesus went out again beside the sea; and all the crowd gathered about him, and he taught them. And as he passed on, he saw Levi the son of Alphaeus sitting at the tax office, and he said to him, "Follow me." And he rose and followed him. And as he sat at table in his house, many tax collectors and sinners were sitting with Jesus and his disciples; for there were many who followed him. And the scribes of the Pharisees, when they saw that he was eating with sinners and tax collectors, said to his disciples, "Why does he eat with the tax collectors and sinners?" And when Jesus heard it, he said to them, "Those who are well have no need of a physician, but those who are sick; I came not to call the righteous, but sinners."

The Gospel of the Lord.

January 19

You Shall Be Vindicated

Daily Bread

Child of God, I may not know how many charges the enemies are brining against you. I don't even know how many cases that are hanging on your neck. You are the only one that knows how many people you are indebted to. No matter how many they may be I am here to announce to you that your period of condemnation is over! God has come to vindicate you. He has come to cancelled evil charges against you.

Isaiah 62:1-5 declares, "For Zion's sake I will not keep silent, and for Jerusalem's sake I will not rest until her vindication goes forth as brightness, and her salvation as a burning torch. The nations shall see your vindication and all the kings your glory."

Child of God, you are blessed! Imagine, God is saying that He will not rest until you are vindicated. That shows how precious you are in the sight of God. God will not rest until all the charges they are bringing against you are cancelled. He will not rest until your lost glory is restored.

Then, "you shall be called by a new name which the mouth of the Lord will give." Just as Isaiah 43:1-2"Fear not, for I have redeemed you; I have called *you* by your name; You *are* Mine. When you pass through the waters, I *will be* with you; And through the rivers, they shall not overflow you. When you walk through the fire, you shall not be burned." All the evil names you have inherited either in your home or in your linage are hereby cancelled in Jesus name! Rejoice for God is blessing you with a new name.

With this new name, "You shall be a crown of beauty in the hand of the Lord, and a royal diadem in the hand of your God." As long as you are in God's hand you are secured. As Zechariah 2:8 declares, He who touches you touches the apple of His eye." You are indeed a crown of beauty in God's hand. God will continue to protect and decorate you.

As God decorates you, "You shall no more be termed Forsaken, and your land shall no more be termed Desolate; but you shall be called My delight and your land Married; for the Lord delights in you, and your land shall be married.

What happened at Cana in Galilee will happen in

all your celebrations. In John 2:1-11 our Lord Jesus Christ attended a marriage at Cana in Galilee where he turned water into wine. Imagine if you were the couple, how will you feel?

And that is what God is promising you when He declares, "For as a young man marries a virgin, so shall your sons marry you, and as the bridegroom rejoices over the bride, so shall your God rejoice over you." This is good news!

God is rejoicing over you! After the baptism of our Lord Jesus Christ, the Father's Voice was heard, saying, "This is My beloved Son, in whom I am well pleased." See how God the Father is rejoicing over His Son our Lord Jesus Christ. This is the same way God will rejoice over you.

From today your life will bring glory to God. As Matthew 5:14-16 "You are the light of the world. A city that is set on a hill cannot be hidden… Let your light so shine before men, that they may see your good works and glorify your Father in heaven." As your life continues to bring glory to God it shall be well with you in Jesus name – Amen!

Happy Second Sunday in Ordinary Time!

Daily Readings:
SUNDAY OF THE SECOND SUNDAY IN ORDINARY TIME

Entrance Antiphon   Ps 66:4
All the earth shall bow down before you, O God, and shall sing to you shall sing to your name, O Most High!

Collect
Almighty ever-living God, who govern all things, both in heaven and on earth, mercifully hear the pleading of your people and bestow your peace on our times. Through our Lord Jesus Christ, your Son, who lives and reigns with you in the unity of the Holy Spirit, one God, for ever and ever.

FIRST READING   Isaiah 62:1-5
"The bridegroom rejoices over the bride."
For Zion's sake I will not keep silent, and for Jerusalem's sake I will not rest until her vindication goes forth as brightness, and her salvation as a burning torch. The nations shall see your vindication, and all the kings your glory; and you shall be called by a new name which the mouth of the Lord will give. You shall be a crown of beauty in

the hand of the Lord, and a royal diadem in the hand of your God. You shall no more be termed Forsaken, and your land shall no more be termed Desolate; but you shall be called My delight is in her, and your land Married; for the Lord delights in you, and your land shall be married. For as a young man marries a virgin, so shall your sons marry you, and as the bridegroom rejoices over the bride, so shall your God rejoice over you.
The word of the Lord.

RESPONSORIAL PSALM:
Psalm 96:1-2a.2b-3.7-8a.9-10a and c (R. cf. 3)
R. Tell among all the peoples the wonders of the Lord.
O sing a new song to the Lord;
sing to the Lord, all the earth.
O sing to the Lord; bless his name. R.

Proclaim his salvation day by day.
Tell among the nations his glory,
and his wonders among all the peoples. R.

Give the Lord, you families of peoples,
give the Lord glory and power;
give the Lord the glory of his name. R.

Worship the Lord in holy splendour.
O tremble before him, all the earth.
Say to the nations, "The Lord is king."
He will judge the peoples in fairness. R.

SECOND READING   1 Corinthians 12:4-11

"One and the same Spirit who apportions to each one individually as he wills."

There are varieties of gifts, but the same Spirit; and there are varieties of service, but the same Lord; and there are varieties of working, but it is the same God who inspires them all in everyone. To each is given the manifestation of the Spirit for the common good. To one is given through the Spirit the utterance of wisdom, and to another the utterance of knowledge according to the same Spirit, to another faith by the same Spirit, to another gifts of healing by the one Spirit, to another the working of miracles, to another prophecy, to another the ability to distinguish between spirits, to another various kinds of tongues, to another the interpretation of tongues. All these are inspired by one and the same Spirit, who apportions to each one individually as he wills.

The word of the Lord.

Gospel Acclamation: 2 Thessalonians 2:14
V. Alleluia. R. Alleluia. V. God has called us through the Gospel, to obtain the glory of our Lord Jesus Christ. R. Alleluia.

GOSPEL   **John 2:1-11**
"This, the first of his signs, Jesus did at Cana in Galilee."

There was a marriage at Cana in Galilee, and the mother of Jesus was there; Jesus also was invited to the marriage, with his disciples. When the wine failed, the mother of Jesus said to him, "They have no wine." And Jesus said to her, "O woman, what is that to you or to me? My hour has not yet come." His mother said to the servants, "Do whatever he tells you." Now six stone jars were standing there, for the Jewish rites of purification, each holding twenty or thirty gallons. Jesus said to them, "Fill the jars with water." And they filled them up to the brim. He said to them, "Now draw some out, and take it to the steward of the feast." So they took it. When the steward of the feast tasted the water now become wine, and did not know where it came from (though the servants who had drawn the water knew), the steward of the feast called the bridegroom and said to him, "Every man serves the good wine first; and

when men have drunk freely, then the poor wine; but you have kept the good wine until now." This, the first of his signs, Jesus did at Cana in Galilee, and manifested his glory; and his disciples believed in him.
The Gospel of the Lord.

Prayer over the Offerings
Grant us, O Lord, we pray, that we may participate worthily in these mysteries, for whenever the memorial of this sacrifice is celebrated the work of our redemption is accomplished. Through Christ our Lord.

Communion Antiphon
You have prepared a table before me, and how precious is the chalice that quenches my thirst.

Or: 1 Jn 4:16
We have come to know and to believe in the love that God has for us.

Prayer after Communion
Pour on us, O Lord, the Spirit of your love, and in your kindness make those you have nourished by this one heavenly Bread one in mind and heart. Through Christ our Lord.

January 20

You Have Been Called by God

Daily Bread

Many are called but few are chosen. Child of God, I want to announce to you that you are among the few chosen ones. God is One that has chosen you! He is the One that has appointed you.

Hebrews 5:1-10 declares, "Every high priest chosen from among men is appointed to act on behalf of men in relation to God, to offer gifts and sacrifices for sins. He can deal gently with the ignorant and wayward, since he himself is beset with weakness. Because of this he is bound to offer sacrifice for his own sins as well as for those of the people." Just like other high priests God has chosen you from among men. He has appointed you to act on behalf of others.

You are lucky for you did not choose yourself, for "one does not take the honour upon himself, but he is called by God, just as Aaron was. So also Christ did not exalt himself to be made a high priest, but was appointed by him who said to him, "You are my Son, today I have begotten you"; as he says also in another place, "You are a priest for ever, according to the order of Melchizedek."

That is exactly what our Lord Jesus Christ meant in John 15:16 where he told his disciples, "You did not choose Me, but I chose you and appointed you that you should go and bear fruit, and *that* your fruit should remain, that whatever you ask the Father in My name He may give you." Your vocation and your calling is everlasting, a priest forever like Melchizedek of old. As you continue to enjoy your vocation it shall be well with you in Jesus name – Amen!

Blessed Michael Iwene Tansi – Pray for Us!

Daily Readings:
MONDAY OF THE SECOND WEEK IN ORDINARY TIME

FIRST READING: Hebrews 5:1-10
"Although he was a Son, he learned obedience through what he suffered."
Every high priest chosen from among men is

appointed to act on behalf of men in relation to God, to offer gifts and sacrifices for sins. He can deal gently with the ignorant and wayward, since he himself is beset with weakness. Because of this he is bound to offer sacrifice for his own sins as well as for those of the people. And one does not take the honour upon himself, but he is called by God, just as Aaron was. So also, Christ did not exalt himself to be made a high priest, but was appointed by him who said to him, "You are my Son, today I have begotten you"; as he says also in another place, "You are a priest for ever, according to the order of Melchizedek." In the days of his flesh, Jesus offered up prayers and supplications, with loud cries and tears, to him who was able to save him from death, and he was heard for his godly fear. Although he was a Son, he learned obedience through what he suffered; and being made perfect he became the source of eternal salvation to all who obey him, being designated by God a high priest according to the order of Melchizedek.

The word of the Lord

RESPONSORIAL PSALM
Psalm 110:1, 2, 3, 4 (R. 4bc)

R/ You are a priest for ever, in the line of Melchizedek.

The **Lord's** revelation to **my** lord:
"Sit at my right hand,
until I make your foes your footstool."

The **Lord** will send from Sion
your sceptre of power:
rule in the midst of your foes. R/

With you is princely rule
on the day of your power.
In holy splendour, from the womb before the dawn,
I have begotten you. R

The **Lord** has sworn an oath he will not change:
"You are a priest for ever,
in the line of Melchizedek."

Gospel Acclamation: Hebrews 412
V/ **Alleluia. R/ Alleluia.** V/ The word of the Lord is living and active, discerning the thoughts and intentions of the heart. R/Alleluia.

GOSPEL   Mark 2:18-22

"The bridegroom is with them."

At that time: John's disciples and the Pharisees were fasting; and people came and said to him, "Why do John's disciples and the disciples of the Pharisees fast, but your disciples do not fast?" And Jesus said to them, "Can the wedding guests fast while the bridegroom is with them? As long as they have the bridegroom with them, they cannot fast. The days will come, when the bridegroom is taken away from them, and then they will fast in that day. No one sews a piece of unshrunk cloth on an old garment; if he does, the patch tears away from it, the new from the old, and a worse tear is made. And no one puts new wine into old wineskins; if he does, the wine will burst the skins, and the wine is lost, and so are the skins; but new wine is for fresh skins."

The Gospel of the Lord.

JANUARY 21
GOD WILL BLESS AND MULTIPLY YOU

Daily Bread

Today is a day of blessing. God has come to bless you. He has come to multiply you. He has come to restore your greatness and fruitfulness. You will never be under a curse again and you will not be stagnated again!

Hebrew 6:13-20 declares, "For when God made a promise to Abraham, since he had no one greater by whom to swear, he swore by himself, saying, "Surely I will bless you and multiply you." Child of God, the Lord God will surely bless you! He will multiply you. He will grant you divine increase!

The first mandate God gave to man after creation is the mandate to be fruitful and multiply. In Genesis 1:28 after creating them male and female the Lord God blessed them and said to them, "Be fruitful and multiply; fill the earth and subdue it; have dominion over the fish of the sea, over the birds of the air, and over every living thing that moves on the earth."

Child of God, the yoke of barrenness and stagnation is hereby cancelled. Your fruitfulness is restored! God bless you as you continue to multiply in Jesus name – Amen!

St. Agnes – Pray for Us!

Daily Readings:
TUESDAY OF THE SECOND WEEK IN ORDINARY TIME

FIRST READING: Hebrews 6:10-20
We have this hope as a sure and steadfast anchor of the soul.

Brethren: God is not so unjust as to overlook your work and the love which you showed for his sake in serving the saints, as you still do. And we desire each one of you to show the same earnestness in realizing the full assurance of hope until the end, so that you may not be sluggish, but imitators of those who through faith and patience inherit the promises. For when God made a promise to Abraham, since he had no one greater by whom to swear, he swore by himself, saying, "Surely I will bless you and multiply you." And thus Abraham, having patiently endured,

obtained the promise. Men indeed swear by a greater than themselves, and in all their disputes an oath is final for confirmation. So when God desired to show more convincingly to the heirs of the promise the unchangeable character of his purpose, he interposed with an oath, so that through two unchangeable things, in which it is impossible that God should prove false, we who have fled for refuge might have strong encouragement to seize the hope set before us. We have this as a sure and steadfast anchor of the soul, a hope that enters into the inner shrine behind the curtain, where Jesus has gone as a forerunner on our behalf, having become a high priest for ever according to the order of Melchizedek.
The word of the Lord

RESPONSORIAL PSALM:
Psalm 111:1bc-2, 4-5, 9 and 10c (R. 5b)
R: The Lord keeps his covenant ever in mind.
I will praise the Lord with all my heart,
in the meeting of the just and the assembly.
Great are the works of the **Lord,**
to be pondered by all who delight in them. R

He has given us a memorial of his wonders.
The **Lord** is gracious and merciful.

He gives food to those who fear him;
keeps his covenant ever in mind. R

He has sent redemption to his people,
and established his covenant for ever.
Holy his name, to be feared.
His praise endures for ever! R

Gospel Acclamation: **Ephesians 1:17-18**
V. **Alleluia. V. Alleluia.** V. May the Father of our Lord Jesus Christ enlighten the eyes of our hearts that we might know what is the hope to which he has called us. **Alleluia.**

GOSPEL **Mark 2:23-28**
"The sabbath was made for man, not man for the sabbath."
It happened that one Sabbath Jesus was going through the grainfields; and as they made their way his disciples began to pluck heads of grain. And the Pharisees said to him, "Look, why are they doing what is not lawful on the sabbath?" And he said to them, "Have you never read what David did, when he was in need and was hungry, he and those who were with him: how he entered the house of God, when Abiathar was high priest, and ate the

showbread, which it is not lawful for any but the priests to eat, and also gave it to those who were with him?" And he said to them, "The sabbath was made for man, not man for the sabbath; so the Son of man is lord even of the sabbath." ***The Gospel of the Lord.***

January 22

You Are a Priest Forever

Daily Bread

There are so many priests in the world but there is a particular priestly order of Melchizedek. Those who belong to the order of Melchizedek do not marry and they do not have linage or inheritance of their own. They are like the priest Melchizedek.

Who is Melchizedek? Melchizedek, according to Hebrews 7:1-3, 15-17 is the priest of the Most High God. He was the priest that blessed Abraham as he was returning from the slaughter of the kings. It was to him that Abraham apportioned a tenth part of everything.

Melchizedek was described as king of righteousness. He is also king of Salem, that is, king of peace. He is without father or mother or genealogy, and has neither beginning of days nor end of life, but resembling the Son of God he continues a priest forever. Does this not remind you of Roman Catholic Priest who have no wife and no family of their own?

This becomes even more evident when another priest arises in the likeness of Melchizedek, who has become a priest, not according to a legal requirement concerning bodily descent but by the power of an indestructible life. For it is witnessed of him, "You are a priest for ever, according to the order of Melchizedek." Child of God, whatever you have received from God is forever. Your Priesthood is forever! Your marital life is forever! Even your salvation and your redemption is forever in Jesus name!

St. Vincent Pallotti – Pray for Us!

Daily Readings:
WEDNESDAY OF THE SECOND WEEK IN ORDINARY TIME

FIRST READING: Hebrews 7:1-3, 15-17

"You are a priest for ever, according to the order of Melchizedek."

Brethren: Melchizedek, king of Salem, priest of the Most High God, met Abraham returning from the slaughter of the kings and blessed him; and to him Abraham apportioned a tenth part of everything. He is first, by translation of his name, king of righteousness, and then he is also king of Salem, that is, king of peace. He is without father or mother or genealogy, and has neither beginning of days nor end of life, but resembling the Son of God he continues a priest for ever. This becomes even more evident when another priest arises in the likeness of Melchizedek, who has become a priest, not according to a legal requirement concerning bodily descent but by the power of an indestructible life. For it is witnessed of him, "You are a priest for ever, according to the order of Melchizedek."

RESPONSORIAL PSALM:
Psalm 110:1, 2,3, 4 (R. 4bc)
You are a priest for ever, in the line of Melchizedek.
The **Lord's** revelation to **my** lord:
"Sit at my right hand,
until I make your foes
your footstool." R

The **Lord** will send from Sion
your sceptre of power:
rule in the midst of your foes. R

With you is princely rule
on the day of your power.

In holy splendour, from the womb before the dawn,
I have begotten you. R

The **Lord** has sworn an oath he will not change:
"You are a priest forever,
in the line of Melchizedek."

Gospel Acclamation: Matthew 4:23
V. Alleluia. **R.** Alleluia. V. Jesus was preaching the Gospel of the kingdom and healing every infirmity among the people. **V.** Alleluia.

GOSPEL   Mark 3:1-6
"Is it lawful on the sabbath to save life or to kill?"
At that time: Again, Jesus entered the synagogue, and a man was there who had a withered hand. And they watched him, to see whether he would heal him on the sabbath, so that they might accuse him. And he said to the man who had the withered hand, "Come here." And he said to them, "Is it lawful on the sabbath to do good or to do harm, to save life or to kill?" But they were silent. And he looked around at them with anger, grieved at their hardness of heart, and said to the man, "Stretch out your hand." He stretched it out, and his hand was restored. The Pharisees went out, and immediately held counsel

with the Herodians against him, how to destroy him.
The Gospel of the Lord.

JANUARY 23

JESUS WILL SURELY SAVE YOU!

Daily Bread

Child of God, you have a Saviour – His name is Jesus! You have a Liberator – His name is Jesus! You have a Healer – His name is Jesus! You equally have a Redeemer – His name is Jesus! He is the only One that can save you. And He will surely save you!

Before the birth of our Lord Jesus Christ, His true identity as our Saviour, was revealed to Joseph in a dream. In the gospel of Matthew 1:21 the Angel told Joseph in a dream, "You shall call His name Jesus, for He will save His people from their sins." Jesus is not only coming to save us from sin, He is also coming to save us from bondage, from the kingdom and forces of darkness. He is coming to save us from the hands of our enemies.

The book of Hebrews 7:25-26 further affirms that Jesus can save us. "Brethren: Jesus is able for all time to save those who draw near to God through him, since he always lives to make intercession for them. For it was fitting that we should have such a high priest, holy, blameless, unstained, separated from sinners, exalted above the heavens."

Child of God, Indeed, our Lord Jesus Christ is able to save you from bondage and captivities! He will surely save you from your sinful life and from the hands of your enemies. And it shall be well with you in Jesus name – Amen!

St. Emerentiana – Pray for us!

Daily Readings: Thursday of the Second Week
FIRST READING : Hebrews 7:25 – 8:6

He offered sacrifices when he offered up himself. Brethren: Jesus is able for all time to save those who draw near to God through him, since he always lives to make intercession for them. For it was fitting that we should have such a high priest, holy, blameless, unstained, separated from sinners, exalted above the heavens. He has no need, like those high priests, to offer sacrifices daily, first for his own sins and then for those of the people; he did this once for all when he offered up himself. Indeed, the law appoints men in their weakness as high priests, but the word of the oath, which came later than the law, appoints a Son

who has been made perfect for ever. Now the point in what we are saying is this: we have such a high priest, one who is seated at the right hand of the throne of the Majesty in heaven, a minister in the sanctuary and the true tent which is set up not by man but by the Lord. For every high priest is appointed to offer gifts and sacrifices; hence it is necessary for this priest also to have something to offer. Now if he were on earth, he would not be a priest at all, since there are priests who offer gifts according to the law. They serve a copy and shadow of the heavenly sanctuary; for when Moses was about to erect the tent, he was instructed by God, saying, "See that you make everything according to the pattern which was shown you on the mountain." But as it is, Christ has obtained a ministry which is as much more excellent than the old as the covenant he mediates is better, since it is enacted on better promises.
The word of the Lord.

RESPONSORIAL PSALM:
Psalm 40:7-8a, 8b-9, 10, 17 (R. see 8a, 9a)
R/ See, I have come, Lord, to do your will.
You delight not in sacrifice and offerings,
but in an open ear.

You do not ask for holocaust and victim.
Then I said, "See, I have come." R

In the scroll of the book it stands written of me:
"I delight to do your will, O my God;
your instruction lies deep within me." R

Your justice I have proclaimed
in the great assembly.
My lips I have not sealed;
you know it, O **Lord. R**

O let there be rejoicing and gladness
for all who seek you.
Let them ever say, "The **Lord** is great,"
who long for your salvation. R

Gospel Acclamation: 2 Timothy 1:10
V. Alleluia. R. Alleluia. V. Our Saviour Christ Jesus abolished death and brought life and immortality to light through the Gospel. **R. Alleluia.**

GOSPEL
"The unclean spirits cried out, 'You are the Son of God.' And he strictly ordered them not to make him known."

At that time: Jesus withdrew with his disciples to the sea, and a great multitude from Galilee followed; also from Judea and Jerusalem and Idumea and from beyond the Jordan and from about Tyre and Sidon a great multitude, hearing all that he did, came to him. And he told his disciples to have a boat ready for him because of the crowd, lest they should crush him; for he had healed many, so that all who had diseases pressed upon him to touch him. And whenever the unclean spirits saw him, they fell down before him and cried out, "You are the Son of God." And he strictly ordered them not to make him known.
The Gospel of the Lord.

January 24

You Are a Covenantal Child

Daily Bread

Are you aware that you are a covenantal child? Do you even know that our God is a Covenant keeping God? Are you ready to renew your covenant with God? Oh yes, your covenant with God is about to be renewed.

Hebrew 8:8-13 declares, "The days will come, says the Lord, when I will establish a new covenant with the house of Israel and with the house of Judah..." Child of God, today is a day you will live to remember. On this very day you shall enter into a new covenant with the Most High God.

But before then begin to renounce evil covenant. Separate yourself from any covenant that does not bring glory to God. Pray against any covenant that is not of God. Begin to pray for the new covenant.

What is this new covenant all about? The Lord God defines the new covenant thus, "This is the covenant that I will make with the house of Israel after those days, says the Lord: I will put my laws into their minds, and write them on their hearts, and I will be their God, and they shall be my people."

Child of God begin to rejoice! Begin to celebrate! The Lord has accepted to be your God. You are now among God's chosen people. With this new covenant God will be merciful towards you. He will remember your sins and your iniquities no more. And it shall be well with you in Jesus name – Amen!

St. Francis de Sales – Pray for us!

Daily Readings:
FRIDAY OF THE 2ND WEEK IN ORDINARY TIME

FIRST READING HEBREWS 8:6-13

Brethren: As it is, Christ has obtained a ministry which is as much more excellent than the old as the covenant he mediates is better, since it is enacted on better promises. For if that first covenant had been faultless, there would have been no occasion for a second. For he finds fault with them when he says: "The days will come, says the Lord, when I will establish a new covenant with the house of Israel and with the house of Judah; not like the covenant that I made with their fathers on the day when I took them by the hand to lead them out of the land of Egypt; for they did not continue in my covenant, and so I paid no heed to them, says the Lord. This is the covenant that I will make with the house of Israel after those days, says the Lord: I will put my laws into their minds, and write them on their hearts, and I will be their God, and they shall be my people. And they shall not teach everyone his fellow or every one his brother, saying, 'Know the Lord.' for all shall know me, from the least of them to the greatest. For I will be merciful toward their iniquities, and I will remember their sins no more." In speaking of a new covenant he treats the first as obsolete. And what is becoming obsolete and growing old is ready to vanish away. *The word of the Lord.*

RESPONSORIAL PSALM: Psalm 85:8 and 10, 11-12, 13-14 (R. 11a)
R/ Merciful love and faithfulness have met.

Let us see, O **Lord,** your mercy,
and grant us your salvation.
His salvation is near for those who fear him,
and his glory will dwell in our land. R

Merciful love and faithfulness have met;
justice and peace have kissed.
Faithfulness shall spring from the earth,
and justice look down from heaven. R

Also the **Lord** will bestow his bounty,
and our earth shall yield its increase.
Justice will march before him,
and guide his steps on the way. R

Gospel Acclamation: 2 Corinthians 5:19
V. **Alleluia.** R. **Alleluia.** V God was in Christ reconciling the world to himself, and entrusting to us the message of reconciliation. R. Alleluia.

GOSPEL   Mark 3:13-19
He called to him those whom he desired to be with him.

At that time: Jesus went up on the mountain, and called to him those whom he desired; and they came to him. And he appointed twelve, to be with him, and to be sent out to preach and have authority to cast out demons: Simon whom he surnamed Peter; Janies the son of Zebedee and John the brother of James, whom he surnamed Boanerges, that is, sons of thunder; Andrew, and Philip, and Bartholomew,

and Matthew, and Thomas, and James the son of Alphaeus, and Thaddaeus, and Simon the Cananaean, and Judas Iscariot, who betrayed him.
The Gospel of the Lord

January 25
Your Past is Over!

Daily Bread

I may not know how sinful you may. I don't even need to know the kind of atrocities you must have committed but I want to let you know that your past is over! As long as you are ready to repent and give your life totally to Jesus Christ, your sins will be forgiven and will be remembered no more.

Today happens to be the feast of the Conversion of St. Paul. In Acts 22:3-16 St. Paul introduced himself and narrated how he persecuted the early Christians. According to him, "I am a Jew, born at Tarsus in Cilicia, but brought up in this city at the feet of Gamaliel, educated according to the strict manner of the law of our fathers, being zealous for God as you all are this day. I persecuted this Way to the death, binding and delivering to prison both men and women…

On his way Damascus where he wanted to arrest more Christians he was arrested and blinded by our Lord Jesus Christ. This led to his ultimate conversion. After his conversion God not only used him to win more souls into God's kingdom He wrote most of the epistles in the New Testament.

Child of God, as long as the conversion of St. Paul is concerned there is still hope for you!

In Isaiah 1:18-20 the Lord God declares, "Come now, and let us reason together," Says the Lord, "Though your sins are like scarlet, They shall be as white as snow; Though they are red like crimson, They shall be as wool. If you are willing and obedient, You shall eat the good of the land; But if you refuse and rebel, You shall be devoured by the sword" Child of God, with this declaration and the conversion of St. Paul, and above all with your own conversion, I assure you, your sins are forgiven! Your past is over! You are hereby declared free in the name of God the Father, God the Son and God the Holy Spirit – Amen!

St. Paul – Pray for Us!

Daily Readings:
CONVERSION OF ST. PAUL

FIRST READING: Acts 22:3-16

Rise and be baptized, and wash away your sins, calling on the name of Jesus.

In those days: Paul said to the people [in Jerusalem], "I am a Jew, born at Tarsus in Cilicia, but brought up in this city at the feet of Gamaliel, educated according to the strict manner of the law of our fathers, being zealous for God as you all are this day. I persecuted this Way to the death, binding and delivering to prison both men and women, as the high priest and the whole council of elders bear me witness. From them I received letters to the brethren, and I journeyed to Damascus to take those also who were there and bring them in bonds to Jerusalem to be punished. "As I made my journey and drew near to Damascus, about noon a great light from heaven suddenly shone about me. And I fell to the ground and heard a voice saying to me, 'Saul, Saul, why do you persecute me?' "And I answered, 'Who are you, Lord?' "And he said to me, 'I am Jesus of Nazareth whom you are persecuting.' "Now those who were with me saw the light but did not hear the voice of the one who was speaking to me. "And I said, 'What shall I do, Lord?' "And the Lord said to me, 'Rise, and go into Damascus, and there you will be told all that is appointed for you to do.' And when I could not see because of the brightness of that light, I was

led by the hand by those who were with me, and came into Damascus. "And one Ananias, a devout man according to the law, well spoken of by all the Jews who lived there, came to me, and standing by me said to me, 'Brother Saul, receive your sight.' And in that very hour I received my sight and saw him. And he said, 'The God of our fathers appointed you to know his will, to see the Just One and to hear a voice from his mouth; for you will be a witness for him to all men of what you have seen and heard. And now why do you wait? Rise and be baptized, and wash away your sins, calling on his name.'"
The word of the Lord.

RESPONSORIAL PSALM
Psalm 117:1, 2 (R. Mark 16:15)
**R/ Go into all the world and preach the Gospel.
or: Alleluia.**
O praise the Lord, all you nations;
Acclaim him, all you peoples!

For his merciful love has prevailed over us;
and the Lord's faithfulness endures forever. R/

ALLELUIA John 15:16

Alleluia. Alleluia. I chose you from the world that you should go and bear fruit and that your fruit should abide, says the Lord. **Alleluia.**

GOSPEL Mark 16:15-18

"Go into all the world and preach the Gospel." At that time: [Appearing to the Eleven,] Jesus said to them, "Go into all the world and preach the Gospel to the whole creation. He who believes and is baptised will be saved; but he who does not believe will be condemned. And these signs will accompany those who believe: in my name they will cast out demons; they will speak in new tongues; they will pick up serpents, and if they drink any deadly thing, it will not hurt them; they will lay their hands on the sick, and they will recover."

The Gospel of the Lord.

January 26

Your Period of Weeping is Over!

Daily Bread

Whatever has a beginning must equally have an end. I want to announce to you that your period of weeping and mourning is over! The Lord has come to wipe away your tears. And so, cry no more!

In the book of Nehemiah 8:9-10 "Nehemiah, who was the governor, and Ezra the priest and scribe, and the Levites who taught the people said to all the people, "This day is holy to the Lord your God; do not mourn or weep." For all the people wept when they heard the words of the law. Then he said to them, "Go your way, eat the fat and drink sweet wine and send portions to him for whom nothing is prepared; for this day is holy to our Lord; and do not be grieved, for the joy of the Lord is your strength." Child of God indeed this day is made by the Lord we rejoice and are glad! The Lord has seen your tears and He has come to console you.

In Isaiah 40:1-2 the Lord God declares, "Comfort, yes, comfort My people!" Says your God. "Speak comfort to Jerusalem, and cry out to her, That her warfare is ended, That her iniquity is pardoned; For she has received from the Lord's hand Double for all her sins." Child of God, the Lord said I should comfort you. So, cry no more for your warfare is over! Your period of sorrow is over! No more bitterness!

In the gospel of John 16:20-22 our Lord Jesus Christ told his followers, "Most assuredly, I say to you that you will weep and lament, but the world will rejoice; and you will be sorrowful, but your sorrow will be turned into joy. A woman, when she is in labor, has sorrow because her hour has come; but as soon as she has given birth to the child, she no longer remembers the anguish, for joy that a human being has been born into the world. Therefore you now have sorrow; but I will see you again and your heart will rejoice, and your joy no one will take from you." Child of God, as God restores your joy no one will ever take your joy from you.

The book of Revelation 21:4 states clearly what happens when our Lord Jesus Christ comes "He will wipe away every tear from their eyes, and death shall be no more, neither shall there be mourning, nor crying, nor pain anymore, for the former things have passed away." Our Lord Jesus Christ is coming to wipe away our tears. He is coming to console us. He is our Comforter!

This is exactly the reason while He was anointed by the Holy Spirit as recorded in Luke 4:18 where He declared, "The Spirit of the Lord is upon me, because he has anointed me to preach good news to the poor. He has sent me to proclaim release to the captives and recovering of sight to the blind, to set at liberty those who are oppressed, to proclaim the acceptable year of the Lord." Indeed, our Lord Christ is the Messiah, the Anointed One.

He was anointed in order to release you from captivity. He was anointed to restore your physical and spiritual sight. He was anointed to liberate you from all forms of oppression. With the anointing of our Lord Jesus Christ your period of captivity is over! Your period of bondage is over. Your period of darkness is over! No more sorrow for you. Your joy and your celebration is restored! Rejoice and celebrate for your case is settled!

Happy Third Sunday in Ordinary Time

Daily Readings:
THIRD SUNDAY IN ORDINARY TIME

Entrance **Antiphon**   Cf. Ps 96:1.6
O sing a new song to the Lord; sing to the Lord, all the earth. In his presence are majesty and splendour, strength and honour in his holy place.

Collect
Almighty ever-living God, direct our actions according to your good pleasure, that in the name of your beloved Son we may abound in good works. Through our Lord Jesus Christ, your Son, who lives and reigns with you in the unity of the Holy Spirit, one God, for ever and ever.

FIRST READING   Nehemiah 8:2-4a.5-6.8-10
They read from the book, from the law of God, and they gave the sense.

In those days: Ezra the priest brought the law before the assembly, both men and women and all who could hear with understanding, on the first day of the seventh month. And he read from it facing the square before the Water Gate from early morning until midday, in the presence of the men and the women and those who could understand; and the

ears of all the people were attentive to the book of the law. And Ezra the scribe stood on a wooden pulpit which they had made for the purpose. And Ezra opened the book in the sight of all the people, for he was above all the people; and when he opened it all the people stood. And Ezra blessed the Lord, the great God; and all the people answered, "Amen, Amen," lifting up their hands; and they bowed their heads and worshipped the Lord with their faces to the ground. And Ezra and the Levites read from the book, from the law of God, clearly; and they gave the sense, so that the people understood the reading. And Nehemiah, who was the governor, and Ezra the priest and scribe, and the Levites who taught the people said to all the people, "This day is holy to the Lord your God; do not mourn or weep." For all the people wept when they heard the words of the law. Then he said to them, "Go your way, eat the fat and drink sweet wine and send portions to him for whom nothing is prepared; for this day is holy to our Lord; and do not be grieved, for the joy of the Lord is your strength."
The word of the Lord.

RESPONSORIAL PSALM
Psalm 19:8.9.10.15 (R. cf. John 6:63c)

R. **Your words, O Lord, are Spirit and life.**
The law of the Lord is perfect;
it revives the soul.
The decrees of the Lord are steadfast;
they give wisdom to the simple. R.

The precepts of the Lord are right;
they gladden the heart.
The command of the Lord is clear;
it gives light to the eyes. R.

The fear of the Lord is pure,
abiding forever.
The judgements of the Lord are true;
they are, all of them, just. R.

May the spoken words of my mouth,
the thoughts of my heart,
win favour in your sight, O Lord,
my rock and my redeemer! R.

SECOND READING   1 Corinthians 12:12-30
You are the body of Christ and individually members of it.

Brethren: Just as the body is one and has many members, and all the members of the body, though many, are one body, so it is with Christ. For by one Spirit we were all baptised into one body - Jews or Greeks, slaves or free - and all were made to drink of one Spirit. For the body does not consist of one member but of many. If the foot should say, "Because I am not a hand, I do not belong to the body," that would not make it any less a part of the body. And if the ear should say, "Because I am not an eye, I do not belong to the body," that would not make it any less a part of the body. If the whole body were an eye, where would be the hearing? If the whole body were an ear, where would be the sense of smell? But as it is, God arranged the organs in the body, each one of them, as he chose. If all were a single organ, where would the body be? As it is, there are many parts, yet one body. The eye cannot say to the hand, "I have no need of you," nor again the head to the feet, "I have no need of you." On the contrary, the parts of the body which seem to be weaker are indispensable, and those parts of the body which we think less honourable we invest with the greater honour, and our unpresentable parts are treated with greater modesty, which our more presentable parts do not require. But God has so adjusted the body, giving the greater honour to the inferior part, that there may be no discord in the body, but that the members may

have the same care for one another. If one member suffers, all suffer together; if one member is honoured, all rejoice together. Now you are the body of Christ and individually members of it. And God has appointed in the Church first apostles, second prophets, third teachers, then workers of miracles, then healers, helpers, administrators, speakers in various kinds of tongues. Are all apostles? Are all prophets? Are all teachers? Do all work miracles? Do all possess gifts of healing? Do all speak with tongues? Do all interpret?
The word of the Lord.

ALLELUIA   Cf.   Luke 4:18
V. Alleluia. **R.** Alleluia.
V. The Lord has sent me to preach good news to the poor, to proclaim release to the captives. **R.** Alleluia.

GOSPEL   Luke 1:1-4; 4:14-21
"Today this Scripture has been fulfilled."
Inasmuch as many have undertaken to compile a narrative of the things which have been accomplished among us, just as they were delivered to us by those who from the beginning were eyewitnesses and ministers of the word, it seemed good to me also, having followed all things closely

for some time past, to write an orderly account for you, most excellent Theophilus, that you may know the truth concerning the things of which you have been informed. At that time: Jesus returned in the power of the Spirit into Galilee, and a report concerning him went out through all the surrounding country. And he taught in their synagogues, being glorified by all. And he came to Nazareth, where he had been brought up; and he went to the synagogue, as was his custom, on the sabbath day. And he stood up to read; and there was given to him the Book of the Prophet Isaiah. He opened the book and found the place where it was written: "The Spirit of the Lord is upon me, because he has anointed me to preach good news to the poor. He has sent me to proclaim release to the captives and recovering of sight to the blind, to set at liberty those who are oppressed, to proclaim the acceptable year of the Lord." And he closed the book, and gave it back to the attendant, and sat down; and the eyes of all in the synagogue were fixed on him. And he began to say to them, "Today this Scripture has been fulfilled in your hearing."

The Gospel of the Lord.

Prayer over the Offerings
Accept our offerings, O Lord, we pray, and in sanctifying them grant that they may profit us for salvation.
Through Christ our Lord.

Communion Antiphon   Cf. Ps 34:6
Look towards the Lord and be radiant; let your faces not be abashed.

Or: Jn. 8:12
I am the light of the world, says the Lord; whoever follows me will not walk in darkness, but will have the light of life.

Prayer after Communion
Grant, we pray, almighty God, that, receiving the grace by which you bring us to new life, we may always glory in your gift.
Through Christ our Lord.

January 27
As You Wait for Christ You will be Saved

Daily Bread

They that put their trust in the Lord are like Mount Zion that cannot be shaken and they that wait for the Lord shall renew their strength! Child of God as you wait for the Lord your will not wait in vain.

Hebrews 9:24-28 For Christ has entered, not into a sanctuary made with hands, a copy of the true one, but into heaven itself, now to appear in the presence of God on our behalf. Nor was it to offer himself repeatedly, as the high priest enters the Holy Place yearly with blood not his own; for then he would have had to suffer repeatedly since the foundation of the world. But as it is, he has appeared once for all at the end of the age to put away sin by the sacrifice of himself. And just as it is appointed for men to die once, and after that comes judgment, so Christ, having been offered once to bear the sins of many, will appear a second time, not to deal with sin but to save those who are eagerly waiting for him.

Indeed, our Lord Jesus Christ has come to save those who are eagerly waiting for Him. Child of God, as you wait for the Lord He will not only renew your strength, He will surely save you and it shall be well with you in Jesus name – Amen!

St. Angela Merci – Pray for Us!

Daily Readings:
MONDAY OF THE THIRD WEEK IN ORDINARY TIME

FIRST READING   Hebrews 9:15, 24-28

He has been offered once to bear the sins of many; he will appear a second time to those who are eagerly waiting for him.

Brethren: Christ is the mediator of a new covenant, so that those who are called may receive the promised eternal inheritance, since a death has occurred which redeems them from the transgressions under the first covenant. For Christ has entered, not into a sanctuary made with hands, a copy of the true one, but into heaven itself, now to appear in the presence of God on our behalf. Nor was it to offer himself repeatedly, as the high priest enters the Holy Place yearly with blood not his own; for then he would have had to suffer repeatedly since the foundation of the world. But as it is, he has appeared once for all at the end of the age to put away sin by the sacrifice of himself. And just as it is appointed for men to die once, and after that comes judgement, so Christ, having been offered once to bear the sins of many, will appear a second time, not to deal with sin but to save those who are eagerly waiting for him.

RESPONSORIAL PSALM
Psalm 98:1, 2-3ab, 3cd-4, 5-6 (R. 1ab)
R/. O sing a new song to the Lord, for he has worked wonders.
O sing a new song to the Lord,
for he has worked wonders.
His right hand and his holy arm
have brought salvation, R

The **Lord** has made known his salvation,
has shown his deliverance to the nations.
He has remembered his merciful love
and his truth for the house of Israel. R

All the ends of the earth have seen
the salvation of our God.

Shout to the **Lord,** all the earth;
break forth into joyous song,
and sing out your praise. R

Sing psalms to the **Lord** with the harp,
with the harp and the sound of song.
With trumpets and the sound of the horn,
raise a shout before the King, the **Lord. R**

Gospel Acclamation: 2 **Timothy 1:10**
V. Alleluia. R. Alleluia. V. Our Saviour Christ Jesus abolished death and brought life and immortality to light through the Gospel. R. **Alleluia.**

GOSPEL   Mark 3:22-30

"Satan is coming to an end."

At that time: The scribes who came down from Jerusalem said of Jesus, "He is possessed by Beelzebul, and by the prince of demons he casts out the demons." And he called them to him, and said to them in parables, "How can Satan cast out Satan? If a kingdom is divided against itself, that kingdom cannot stand. And if a house is divided against itself, that house will not be able to stand. And if Satan has risen up against himself and is divided, he cannot stand, but is coming to an end. But no one can enter

a strong man's house and plunder his goods, unless he first binds the strong man; then indeed he may plunder his house. "Truly, I say to you, all sins will be forgiven the sons of men, and whatever blasphemies they utter; but whoever blasphemes against the Holy Spirit never has forgiveness, but is guilty of an eternal sin" for they had said, "He has an unclean spirit."
The Gospel of the Lord.

JANUARY 28
YOU WILL DO GOD'S WILL

Daily Bread

God's will is the best thing that can happen to anyone. In the gospel of John 4:34 our Lord Jesus Christ said, "My food is to do the will of Him who sent Me, and to finish His work." You know how important food is to us, human beings. Most of us cannot survive without food. For our Lord Jesus Christ to say that His food is to do God's will that shows that God's will is more delicious than material food.

Hebrew 10:5-10 declares, "Consequently, when Christ came into the world, he said, "Sacrifices and offerings you have not desired, but a body you have prepared for me; in burnt offerings and sin offerings you have taken no pleasure. Then I said, 'Behold, I have come to do your will, O God,' as it is written of me in the roll of the book." Obedience to God's will is far more better than sacrifice.

The Author of the book of Hebrews further declares, "You have neither desired nor taken pleasure in sacrifices and offerings and burnt offerings and sin offerings" then he added, "Behold, I have come to do your will." Child of God, may God grant you the grace to do his will and as you do His will it shall be well with you in Jesus name – Amen!

St. Thomas Aquinas – Pray for Us!

Daily Readings:
TUESDAY OF THIRD WEEK IN ORDINARY TIME

FIRST READING   Hebrews 10:1-10

"Behold, I have come to do your will, O God." Brethren: Since the law has but a shadow of the good things to come instead of the true form of these realities, it can never, by the same sacrifices which are continually offered year after year, make perfect those who draw near. Otherwise, would they not have ceased to be offered? If the worshippers had once been cleansed, they would no longer have any consciousness of sin. But in these sacrifices, there is a reminder of sin year after year. For it is impossible that the blood of bulls and goats should take away sins. Consequently, when Christ came into the world, he said, "Sacrifices and offerings you have not

desired, but a body you have prepared for me; in burnt offerings and sin offerings you have taken no pleasure. Then I said, 'Behold, I have come to do your will, O God,' as it is written of me in the roll of the book." When he said above, "You have neither desired nor taken pleasure in sacrifices and offerings and burnt offerings and sin offerings" (these are offered according to the law), then he added, "Behold, I have come to do your will." He abolishes the first in order to establish the second. And by that will we have been sanctified through the offering of the body of Jesus Christ once for all.
The word of the Lord

RESPONSORIAL PSALM:
Psalm 40:2 and 4ab, 7-8a, 10, 11 (R. see 8a, 9a)
R. I See, I have come, Lord, to do your will.
I waited, I waited for the Lord,
and he stooped down to me;
he heard my cry.
He put a new song into my mouth,
praise of our God. R

You delight not in sacrifice and offerings,
but in an open ear.
You do not ask for holocaust and victim.

Then I said, "See, I have come." R

Your justice I have proclaimed
in the great assembly.
My lips I have not sealed;
you know it, O **Lord. R**

Your saving help I have not hidden in my heart;
of your faithfulness and salvation I have spoken.
I made no secret of your merciful love
and your faithfulness to the great assembly. R

Gospel Acclamation: Matthew 11:25
V. Alleluia. R. Alleluia. V. Blessed are you, Father, Lord of heaven and earth, that you have revealed to little ones the mysteries of the kingdom. R. **Alleluia.**

GOSPEL Mark 3:31-35
"Whoever does the will of God is my brother, and sister, and mother."

At that time: The mother of Jesus and his brethren came; and standing outside they sent to him and called him. And a crowd was sitting about him; and they said to him, "Your mother and your brethren are outside, asking for you." And he replied, "Who are my mother and my brethren?" And looking

around on those who sat about him, he said, "Here are my mother and my brethren! Whoever does the will of God is my brother, and sister, and mother."
The Gospel of the Lord.

January 29

Your Sins Will Be Remembered No More

Daily Bread

Sin is the worst thing that can happen to anyone. A sinner is a slave. In the gospel of John 8:34-36 our Lord Jesus Christ declares, "Most assuredly, I say to you, whoever commits sin is a slave of sin. And a slave does not abide in the house forever, *but* a son abides forever. Therefore, if the Son makes you free, you shall be free indeed.

Hebrews 10:15-18 declares "The Holy Spirit also bears witness to us; for after saying, "This is the covenant that I will make with them after those days, says the Lord: I will put my laws on their hearts, and write them on their minds," then he adds, "I will remember their sins and their misdeeds no more." Where there is forgiveness of sin, there is no longer any offering for sin.

Child of God, no matter how sinful you are with our Lord Jesus Christ there is still hope for you. In

Isaiah 1:18-19 the Lord God declares

"Come now, and let us reason together," Says the Lord," Though your sins are like scarlet, They shall be as white as snow; Though they are red like crimson, They shall be as wool. If you are willing and obedient, You shall eat the good of the land." As you repent and come back to God He will forgive all your sins. He will remember your sins no more and it shall be well with you in Jesus name – Amen!

St. Apollinaris Claudius – Pray for us!

.

Daily Readings:
WEDNESDAY OF THE THIRD WEEK IN ORDINARY TIME

FIRST READING   Hebrews   10:11-18
"He has perfected for all time those who are sanctified."

Every priest stands daily at his service, offering repeatedly the same sacrifices, which can never take away sins. But when Christ had offered for all time a single sacrifice for sins, he sat down at the right hand of God, then to wait until his enemies should be made a stool for his feet. For by a single offering he has perfected for all time those who are sanctified.

And the Holy Spirit also bears witness to us; for after saying, "This is the covenant that I will make with them after those days, says the Lord: I will put my laws on their hearts, and write them on their minds," then he adds, "I will remember their sins and their misdeeds no more." Where there is forgiveness of these, there is no longer any offering for sin.
The word of the Lord.

RESPONSORIAL PSALM
Psalm 110:1, 2, 3, 4 (R. 4bc)

R/ You are a priest for ever, in the line of Melchizedek.

The **Lord's** revelation to my lord:
"Sit at my right hand,
until I make your foes your footstool." R

The **Lord** will send from Sion
your sceptre of power:
rule in the midst of your foes. R

With you is princely rule
on the day of your power.
In holy splendour, from the womb before the dawn,
I have begotten you. R

The **Lord** has sworn an oath he will not change:
"You are a priest forever,
in the line of Melchizedek."

ALLELUIA
V. Alleluia. **R.** Alleluia **V.** The seed is the word of God, and the sower is Christ; all who find him will abide for ever. R. Alleluia.

GOSPEL Mark 4:1-20

"A sower went out to sow."

At that time: Again, Jesus began to teach beside the sea. And a very large crowd gathered about him, so that he got into a boat and sat in it on the sea; and the whole crowd was beside the sea on the land. And he taught them many things in parables, and in his teaching he said to them:

"Listen! A sower went out to sow. And as he sowed, some seed fell along the path, and the birds came and devoured it. Other seed fell on rocky ground, where it had not much soil, and immediately it sprang up, since it had no depth of soil and when the sun rose it was scorched, and since it had no root it withered away. Other seed fell among thorns and the thorns grew up and choked it, and it yielded no grain. And other seeds fell into good soil and brought forth grain, growing up and increasing and yielding thirtyfold and sixtyfold and a hundredfold." And he said, "He who has ears to hear, let him hear."

And when he was alone, those who were about him with the Twelve asked him concerning the parables. And he said to them, "To you has been given the secret of the kingdom of God, but for those outside everything is in parables; so that they may indeed see but not perceive, and may indeed hear but not understand; lest they should turn again, and be forgiven." And he said to them, "Do you not understand this parable? How then will you understand all the parables? The sower sows the word.

And these are the ones along the path, where the word is sown; when they hear, Satan immediately comes and takes away the word which is sown in them. And these in like manner are the ones sown upon rocky ground, who, when they hear the word, immediately receive it with joy; and they have no root in themselves, but endure for a while; then, when tribulation or persecution arises on account of the word, immediately they fall away.

And others are the ones sown among thorns; they are those who hear the word, but the cares of the world, and the delight in riches, and the desire for other things, enter in and choke the word, and it proves unfruitful. But those that were sown upon the good soil are the ones who hear the word and accept it and bear fruit, thirtyfold and sixtyfold and a hundredfold."

January 30
Your God is a Faithful God

Daily Bread

The best thing that can happen to anyone is to be connected to a faithful God. A faithful God is a reliable God. He is a dependable God. A faithful God is covenant keeping God. Child of God, you are about to encounter the Faithful God.

Hebrew 10:19-25 declares, "Brethren, since we have confidence to enter the sanctuary by the blood of Jesus, by the new and living way which he opened for us through the curtain, that is, through his flesh, and since we have a great priest over the house of God, let us draw near with a true heart in full assurance of faith, with our hearts sprinkled clean from an evil conscience and our bodies washed with pure water. Let us hold fast the confession of our hope without wavering, for he who promised is faithful…" our God is a Faithful God!

Indeed, He who promised is faithful. He is the

Covenant Keeping God. He is a reliable God. He will never fail or disappoint you. He will fulfil all the promises He has made to you. And to Him be glory and praise both now and forevermore – Amen!

St. Aidan / Bathildis – Pray for Us!

Daily Readings:
THURSDAY OF THE THIRD WEEK IN ORDINARY TIME

FIRST READING   Hebrews   10:19-25
"Let us holdfast the confession of our hope without wavering, and let us consider how to stir up one another to love."

Brethren, since we have confidence to enter the sanctuary by the blood of Jesus, by the new and living way which he opened for us through the curtain, that is, through his flesh, and since we have a great priest over the house of God, let us draw near with a true heart in full assurance of faith, with our hearts sprinkled clean from an evil conscience and our bodies washed with pure water. Let us hold fast the confession of our hope without wavering, for he who promised is faithful; and let us consider how to stir up one another to love and good works, not

neglecting to meet together, as is the habit of some, but encouraging one another, and all the more as you see the Day drawing near.
The word of the Lord.

RESPONSORIAL PSALM
Psalm 24:1-2, 3-4ab, 5-6 (R. 6)
R/ These are the people who seek your face, O Lord.
The **Lord's** is the earth and its fullness,
the world, and all who dwell in it.
It is he who set it on the seas;
on the rivers he made it firm. R

Who shall climb the mountain of the **Lord?**
Who shall stand in his holy place?
The clean of hands and pure of heart,
whose soul is not set on vain things. R

Blessings from the **Lord** shall he receive,
and right reward from the God who saves him.
Such are the people who seek him,
who seek the face of the God of Jacob. R

ALLELUIA   **Psalm 119:105**
V. Alleluia. **R** Alleluia. **V.** Your word is a lamp for my feet, and a light for my path. **R.** Alleluia.

GOSPEL   Mark 4:21-25

A lamp is brought in to be put on a stand. The measure you give will be the measure you get.

At that time: Jesus said to the crowd, "Is a lamp brought in to be put under a bushel, or under a bed, and not on a stand? For there is nothing hidden, except to be made manifest; nor is anything secret, except to come to light. If any man has ears to hear, let him hear." And he said to them, "Take heed what you hear; the measure you give will be the measure you get, and still more will be given you. For to him who has will more be given; and from him who has not, even what he has will be taken away."
The Gospel of the Lord.

January 31
You Shall Live by Faith

Daily Bread

Faith keeps us alive. The faithful ones are those whose lives are sustained by their faith in the Most High God. Most of those who received their healing through our Lord Jesus Christ were healed because of their unshakable faith in God. For instance our Lord Jesus Christ assured the woman with an issue of Blood, "Daughter, your faith has made you well. Go in peace, and be healed of your affliction." (Mark 5:34)

Hebrews 10:36-39 For you have need of endurance, so that you may do the will of God and receive what is promised. "For yet a little while, and the coming one shall come and shall not tarry; but my righteous one shall live by faith, and if he shrinks back, my soul has no pleasure in him." But we are not of those who shrink back and are destroyed, but of those who have faith and keep their souls." Faith is what sustains the life of a righteous and upright one. Hence, the righteous shall live by faith.

This is exactly what John 3:16 is all about: "For God so loved the world that He gave His only begotten Son, that whoever believes in Him should not perish but have everlasting life."

The gospel of Mark 16:16 also declares, "He who believes and is baptized will be saved; but he who does not believe will be condemned." Child of God, with your faith in Christ Jesus you will not be condemned. You will surely live and it shall be well with you in Jesus name – Amen!

St. John Bosco – Pray for Us!

Daily Readings:
THIRD WEEK IN ORDINARY TIME

FIRST READING   **Hebrews 10:32-39**

You endured a hard struggle. Therefore, do not throw away your confidence.

Brethren: Recall the former days when, after you were enlightened, you endured a hard struggle with sufferings, sometimes being publicly exposed to abuse and affliction, and sometimes being partners with those so treated. For you had compassion on the prisoners, and you joyfully accepted the plundering of your property, since you knew that you

yourselves had a better possession and an abiding one. Therefore, do not throw away your confidence, which has a great reward. For you have need of endurance, so that you may do the will of God and receive what is promised. "For yet a little while, and the coming one shall come and shall not tarry; but my righteous one shall live by faith, and if he shrinks back, my soul has no pleasure in him." But we are not of those who shrink back and are destroyed, but of those who have faith and keep their souls.
The word of the Lord.

RESPONSORIAL PSALM
Psalm 37:3-4, 5-6, 23-24, 39-40 (R. 39a)
R. From the Lord comes the salvation of the just.
Trust in the Lord and do good;
then you will dwell in the land and safely pasture.
Find your delight in the **Lord,**
who grants your heart's desire. R

Commit your way to the **Lord;**
trust in him, and he will act,
and make your uprightness shine like the light,
the justice of your cause like the noon-day sun. R

By the **Lord** are the steps made firm

of one in whose path He delights.
Though he stumble he shall never fall,
for the **Lord** will hold him by the hand. R

But from the Lord comes the salvation of the just,
their stronghold in time of distress.
The **Lord** helps them and rescues them,
rescues and saves them from the wicked:
because they take refuge in him. R

Gospel Acclamation: Matthew 11:25
V. Alleluia. R. Alleluia. V. Blessed are you, Father, Lord of heaven and earth, that you have revealed to little ones the mysteries of the kingdom. **R. Alleluia.**

GOSPEL Mark 4:26-34

A man scatters seed, and while he sleeps it grows, he knows not how.

At that time: Jesus said to the crowds, "The kingdom of God is as if a man should scatter seed upon the ground, and should sleep and rise night and day, and the seed should sprout and grow, he knows not how. The earth produces of itself, first the blade, then the ear, then the full grain in the ear. But when the grain is ripe, at once he puts in the sickle, because the harvest has come." And he said, "With what can we compare the kingdom of God, or what parable shall we use for it? It is like a grain of mustard seed, which, when sown upon the ground, is the smallest of all the seeds on earth; yet when it is sown it grows up and becomes the greatest of all shrubs, and puts forth large branches, so that the birds of the air can make nests in its shade." With many such parables he spoke the word to them, as they were able to hear it; he did not speak to them without a parable, but privately to his own disciples he explained everything.

Made in the USA
Las Vegas, NV
02 April 2025